Decorative Folk Painting

DECORATIVE FOLK PAINTING

 Jean Payne

CASSELL

I dedicate this book to Evie and Marjorie

A CASSELL BOOK

First published 1995
by Cassell
Villiers House
41/47 Strand
London WC2N 5JE

Distributed in the United States
by Sterling Publishing Co., Inc.
387 Park Avenue South, New York, New York 10016-8810

Distributed in Australia
by Capricorn Link (Australia) Pty Ltd
2/13 Carrington Road
Castle Hill
NSW 2154

British Library Cataloguing-in-Publication Data
A catalogue record for this book is available from
the British Library

ISBN 0-304-34391-9

Designed by Sue Clarke
Photography by Martin Norris

Typeset by Litho Link Limited, Welshpool, Powys, Wales
Printed and bound in Hong Kong

Contents

....

Acknowledgments

···

Many thanks to my teacher in Canada, Lilian Lane, and to Mary Stratton for introducing me to tole painting and not telling me what I was letting myself in for! Also to David and Hazel Madder-Smith of Dome Ltd, Guildford, for their continued support and generosity – on my return from Canada they opened the doors of their art store to me, to help me in my search for brushes and paints in the UK.

I would like to thank the following: the art manufacturers Daler-Rowney in Bracknell for their generosity and help in making this book possible (in particular, John Gilboy and Jon Lloyd); Williams and Son in London for generously giving their Folk Art supplies; Andy and Dean of Crowthorne Print Room for their assistance; Ken Ledbury of Crowthorne for his helpful criticism, encouragement and, last but not least, his excellent woodwork;

Fran Piggott for researching the history of folk art; my friends (in particular, Sonja Barrie, Laurie Tubb and John Oak) who said I could do it and provided me with the technology to make sure that I did!

Not forgetting all my students who kept asking me when I was going to write a book, and the brave students who tested the designs – an extra big thank you to the following who helped: Vonnie Fletcher; Gillian Ann Marriner; Leslie Ruth Marriner; Sophie Palm; Margaret Sharp; Valerie Waite; Elaine Whitchelo-Jones.

Thanks also to Petronella Wells for painting the Hindelooper design on the jug (see page 12) and to Simon Griffiths for painting the Buckby can. Finally a thank you to my friends John and Bunty Townsend for letting me use their home and garden for photography.

Introduction

By purchasing this book you have already proved to yourself that you are creative and have the desire to paint, so I hope you enjoy painting the projects as much as I enjoyed designing them for you.

In the preparation of this book I have not only adapted traditional designs, but also created my own with the aid of modern methods and materials. This helps to illustrate the decorative folk painting that evolved in both the Old World and the New. Decorative folk art is popular in North America, in all its forms, as a reminder of things past and as a contrast to the standardized patterns of mechanization.

Decorative folk painting is a diverse art form using a variety of techniques and media; it can be used to adorn both functional and ornamental objects, and enables you to decorate your home with a unique touch, incorporating styles from the past and materials from the present. As you learn the techniques your new-found creativity will bring lasting pleasure, in both the painting itself and the completed work.

HOW TO USE THIS BOOK

This book can be used in two different ways to give you maximum enjoyment.

If you are keen to get started on a project and have some folk painting experience, why not use the reference table (see Fig. 14, page 59) to show you which techniques to read about before plunging into the creative maelstrom!

You may, however, prefer a more leisurely and ordered approach; in which case I have ordered the chapters, as far as possible, so that the techniques are described in sequence and in order of difficulty.

When you use the worksheets, you will see that it is suggested that you photocopy them rather than working direct from the book. It must be stressed, however, that they may be photocopied only for the purpose of practising the brush strokes.

HAPPY PAINTING!

Those of us who already practise decorative folk painting find it completely absorbing, very relaxing and extremely rewarding. We are in a new world, with new friends. We use the same patterns, but invariably that unique touch gives each painting a mark of its own.

All of us are creative and have a need to express that creativity in some form, but we are often held back by our own lack of confidence or fear of being unsuccessful. Decorative folk painting is ideal for beginners without artistic training or inherent drawing ability as the use of patterns creates a high success rate, while those with drawing skills can use their creative talents to the utmost. Both beginners and those with artistic ability will need to discipline themselves from the outset. Many of my students had never painted before but now produce exceptional work. Those who were already watercolour painters at first found it difficult, but soon learnt to adapt to the unique stylized method. You can see examples of students' painting in this book after less than fifty hours in a classroom. Be positive! If they can do it, so can you.

I hope that those of you who have painted before will enjoy using new brush strokes, such as jagged crescent and pointed crescent. The key to success in decorative folk painting is a systematic approach and practice, practice . . . but, above all, have fun!

Note to American readers

The following terminology is used in this book:
kitchen paper: paper towels
polystyrene: styrofoam
retarder: extender
acetate: clear plastic sheet
plastic filler: filler for metal
for reservoir paper use regular paper towel
for membrane paper use tracing paper from a pad

CHAPTER 1

A brief history of folk art

FACT OR FOLKLORE?

Folk art is the term used to describe the native arts and crafts of any particular region. It is a practical, traditional cultural form, handed on between individuals, usually without any formal training. The history of folk art involves both fact and a wealth of folklore and legend. Separating them is sometimes difficult.

I first became intrigued by decorative folk art while living in Canada. I began to trace the influences on folk painting, starting from the current North American art and searching for the roots in the countries that were the original sources. Travelling in the United States of America, I was introduced to the folk art of the Pennsylvania Dutch. Emigration, especially of the German-speaking people ('Dutch' in this instance is a corruption of *Deutsch*), had brought these decorative art forms to America from Europe, where they developed their own unique styles, which are now highly regarded. New England traditions were also significant, but examples are harder to find.

There are many different influences in folk art today, and tracing their origins is not an easy task. Some of the main influences are mentioned here and described later. The tradition of Bauernmalerei began in the Alpine regions of Germany, Austria and Switzerland. Norway produced the painting known as rosemaling, primarily used in interior decoration. In Holland, sailors in the port of Hindeloopen began a tradition of object decoration. Russian folk art and English canal art have also contributed to the world folk art scene.

It has been suggested that some folk art has its origins in gypsy culture. Certainly many of the painters were itinerant and there are similarities between the colourfully painted Romany wagons and more vividly stylized decorative folk art. The castles painted on English barges could have been copied from castles in central Europe and Bavaria. Some of the colours and brush strokes of roses painted on American chairs are reminiscent of the English roses featured on canal boats.

IN THE BEGINNING

From the beginning my attention was drawn to the fact that all the designs of painting as a form of folk art are based on the comma-shaped brush stroke. This brush stroke seems to have evolved from the shape of the leaf of the acanthus (see Fig. 1), an ornamental plant popular for its decorative possibilities. The leaf shape was originally copied as a decorative motif by the Greeks and Romans and used again in the revival of classical forms during the Italian Renaissance. The acanthus plant has been an inspiration for the scroll designs of all European folk art.

The hand-painted decoration of houses, furniture, wooden objects, pottery and metal ware first made its appearance towards the end of the Middle Ages in Europe.

FIG. 1
Example of an acanthus scroll

The heavily ornamented baroque style of architecture and decorative art of the late sixteenth to early eighteenth century included the extensive use of marble in churches and castles. To reflect this style a marbling technique was developed by painters to use as a background on painted furniture. Rococo, a style that originated in France in the early eighteenth century, was elaborate but more graceful. The profuse intermingling of shell shapes, C-scrolls, ribbon forms and irregular acanthus foliation developed in this period. The fantastic ornamentation on the fountains at Versailles shows us a good example. *Rocaille,* the French for rockwork, is a term used in folk painting to describe shell and swirl motifs.

Exploration and trade in the sixteenth century had introduced exotic influences from Asia and the eastern Mediterranean. The tulip, which is a favourite motif in folk art, appeared at this time. Lacquered cabinets and screens were imported from China and Japan to England during the seventeenth and eighteenth centuries, although the popularity of the 'Sheraton' style of painted furniture among the richer and more important people in society was latterly in decline.

FORMS AND SYMBOLISM

Nature is represented in all decorative folk painting, especially in the form of flowers, leaves, fruit and birds. All these forms are symbolic of people's beliefs and hopes, such as for peace and prosperity. The popular wheat spray (see Fig. 2) and pomegranate are symbols of fertility; the pine tree (see Fig. 3) a sign of good luck. The tree of life design (see Fig. 4) originated in the Far East. This is often depicted with lilies growing on the tree, representing peace. In North America the maple is representative of

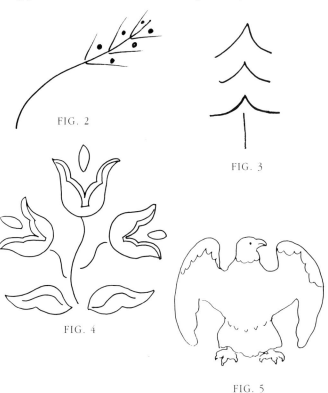

FIG. 2

FIG. 3

FIG. 4

FIG. 5

life's beauty, whereas the eagle (see Fig. 5) symbolizes strength and courage. The dove is a Christian religious motif for the Holy Spirit, representing love and fidelity – with an olive branch the dove represents peace and good news (the dove is incorporated in the Pennsylvanian design in Project 20).

Fruit appears in abundance, grapes and strawberries being particular favourites. Their colour and texture complement each other, as can be seen on the mixed fruit tray in Project 10. Decorating utensils with a pineapple invites sharing and is a symbol denoting friendship and warm hospitality.

Colours also have a special meaning. A great influence is vibrant red, representing the life-giving sun, happiness, hope, passion and nobility. The colour purple, recognized universally as representative of the highest rank, also signifies faith, patience and trust. Green is for spring, the rebirth of nature which brings freshness and fertility, and brown is for mother earth. Blue is for the sky and life-giving air and is a talisman for good health. White symbolizes purity, innocence and birth.

Patterns frequently symbolize ideas. Often used is a border pattern of wavy lines, as can be seen in Project 1, which expresses life itself with all its ups and downs.

GERMANY, AUSTRIA AND SWITZERLAND: PENNSYLVANIA DUTCH

Prior to the end of the seventeenth century the vast majority of immigrants to America came from English stock. By the middle of the eighteenth century, however, a great concentration of German-speaking people had settled in south-eastern Pennsylvania, becoming known as the Pennsylvania Dutch – a corruption of *Deutsch,* as mentioned earlier. These new pioneers were primarily country people who had survived the rigours of the journey from their homeland and the challenges of their new settlements. When time allowed, a desire to bring some colour and decoration into their homes encouraged the settlers to recall the folk patterns and handicrafts that had been familiar to them. Working from memory, with primitive tools, the Pennsylvania Dutch folk artists created designs and patterns that were European in origin but with a very distinctive American influence.

As paints and brushes were practically unobtainable by eighteenth-century settlers, substitutes had to be found. Various shades of brown were made from the

Pennsylvanian red clay and also from onion skins. Cobalt imported from Africa was used to provide blue pigment; indigo derived from the plant of the same name provided a blue dye. Rose petals were scalded to obtain a reddish hue, iris flowers produced purple, saffron gave yellow. Flour or dried milk was used to thicken these paints. For brushes, feathers were used, along with home-made brushes of cat's tail reeds and wisps of straw.

A painting technique that was popular in the early nineteenth century was false graining, for which the artist used corn cobs, sponges, putty or special graining combs. This method of fake wood graining was used to good effect on larger pieces of furniture, such as sideboards and doors.

Another technique popular during this period was smoked decoration. The sooty smoke from a kerosene lamp was blown on to the wet, oil-painted surface of the furniture. An example of this distinctive form of decoration is in the Landis Valley Museum in Lancaster County, Pennsylvania, USA, on a chair dated 1840.

The settlers clung to the traditional patterns and designs from their old homeland in Europe. The tulip, for example, was a firm favourite and frequently used; it was loved because of the easily drawn flower head. It took the place of the lily, symbolizing man's search for God and a promise of bliss in paradise.

Roses and fuchsias were also popular flowers for the folk painters of Pennsylvania. In Project 13 you will see a chest of drawers that I have painted featuring fuchsias.

Birds continued to be a popular subject in their familiar European forms, but the artists in their new environment found fresh and more exotic varieties to depict. The eagle, a native bird of America, became especially favoured after the American Revolution, its image appearing on such diverse objects as pottery, quilts, certificates and butter moulds. Pairs of birds, most often doves, parrots and peacocks, were frequently used as an interesting focal point

FIG. 6

in designs. The peacock (see Fig. 6) was sometimes painted looking backwards at its tail, depicting renewal, since its tail is lost and regrown every year. The thistlefinch, as an eater of seeds from the unwanted thistle, became a symbol of good luck to the farmers. They called the bird 'distelfink' in their effort to pronounce its English name.

The distelfink (see Fig. 7) often appeared as a motif in the decoration of barns, a practice which probably began in the early nineteenth century. The wooden Dutch barn is a unique feature in south-eastern Pennsylvania. The big and colourful geometric designs, known as hex signs, that are still to be seen in this area were initially painted to ward off evil spirits. Hex signs were so named because the original design was a six-pointed star shape with different forms to symbolize events or superstitions. For example, the heart represented love and marriage, the eagle strength, the distelfink good luck and the unicorn virtue and piety. I have incorporated the heart form in Project 4.

FIG. 7

Decorative folk art is commonly known as tole painting in North America. This name derives from the French *tole peinte* (meaning painted tin), which in turn comes from the Latin *taule* (sheet of iron). In the nineteenth century, tin was brought to the North American continent from the tin mines in Cornwall. There is a very distinct resemblance between the brush strokes used to decorate English canal ware and those on Pennsylvania Dutch items associated with this trade.

Pedlars sold the tin ware (or 'poor man's silver') all along the eastern coastline. Tin utensils replaced wood and leather ones and were undecorated until japanned goods became fashionable. (Japanning was a process which gave the thin iron sheets a glossy, semi-transparent finish.) An advantage of this vogue was that japanning served to prevent rusting. Whole families would decorate tin ware with flowers and scenes of their homeland, making this folk art authentically North American. If the settlers did not decorate their own wares, there were plenty of itinerant painters, or 'flowerers' as they were called, who would oblige. The coffee pot in particular, always an essential item in American households, benefited from this fashion. Examples of early American tin ware show that vermilion, dull olive green and bright yellow and white formed the standard colour combination.

All this artistic activity, of course, took place in the context of a strong Christian background. Various religious groups were involved, including Quakers and Mennonites. One of the interesting offshoots of the Mennonites is the Amish farming community, which has a tradition of painting utility objects still continued today.

BAVARIA: BAUERNMALEREI

The decorative folk art that evolved in the Alpine regions of Germany, Austria and Switzerland is known as Bauernmalerei – literally farmer painting. Its name indicates its early peasant origins as the painting was originally done by untrained artists whose techniques were handed down from father to son. Bauernmalerei evolved from several regional styles, but followed the prevailing artistic tastes of the period.

During the Renaissance, geometric designs, often incorporating stencil techniques on natural wood grain, were used to decorate furniture and wooden objects. From the seventeenth century onwards the technique Kleistermalerei was employed in furniture painting; based on the use of a paste which was applied in the form of false graining or marbling, it was used to enhance the inferior soft pine wood furniture and to preserve it. Interest in this cheerful, stylized decoration spread and it became fashionable to commission the illustration of special pieces of furniture to celebrate important events. Designs of flowers, birds and scrolls were used on wedding chests and cradles. Gothic script, recording family names and events, was embellished with motifs to decorate both furniture and other objects (this was known as Fractur drawing).

The baroque period in the eighteenth century gave rise to colourful and elaborate arrangements with stiff, stylized flowers and fruit. This form of decoration was popular in Switzerland, characterized by bright colourful backgrounds and flowers painted in reds, yellows and blues. Birds and fruit, especially bunches of grapes, enhanced by striking borders often appear in this style.

This was followed in the late nineteenth century by the

Three folk art styles: Bauernmalerei – the chair; Pennsylvania Dutch – the coffee tin; and Russian florals – the japanned tray

adoption of rococo styles. Here the designs were less symmetrical; marbling and 'swirl' techniques were used with less colour but increasingly ornate flower designs.

A simplified style known as Biedermeier appeared in the early twentieth century. Alpine scenes depicting everyday peasant life, with mountains, churches, castles and animals, were painted on all kinds of furniture and wooden objects. Romantic ribbons, wreaths of roses and bows were added. This taste was favoured by the *nouveaux riches*, but in a more brightly coloured, opulent, decorative style. The scenes depicted are not realistic as there is no true perspective. This is stylized painting by an artist having fun. Alpine decorative folk art has evolved with elements of all these different styles, and remains distinctive.

Bauernmalerei style is shown on the milk can in Project 11 with the familiar design of bird and tulips. Project 5, the spinner's chair, shows chrysanthemums and daisies in a Bauernmalerei style more akin to the Biedermeier period.

NORWAY: ROSEMALING

In the mid-eighteenth to late nineteenth century, rosemaling (rose painting), Norway's unique decorative painting, was at its peak.

The original patterns for rosemaling arose from the rococo scrolls of carving in the wooden churches. The rose-shaped scrolls were lovingly copied as the rose has always been a symbol of love and beauty and figures significantly in all art. Early carvings also contained acanthus leaf forms which had been favoured in the Renaissance period. Wealthy merchants and farmers were able to hire town painters to decorate their homes, but when the popularity of rosemaling spread to the isolated villages, peasant farming families began to paint their own interiors and furniture. The early painting of the country people was quite primitive, as they used their fingers, hands or a home-made brush with free and instinctive movements, giving self-expression to their artistry. Small wooden articles, such as ale bowls, boxes, tankards and small chests, were decorated, then furniture, walls and ceilings. Nordic myths and biblical stories were included in the designs, with sayings and messages worked in to indicate ownership. Special occasions and festivals were celebrated with a message painted as a border on the rim of bowls and platters.

Three particular areas developed their own style of rosemaling, namely Telemark, Hallingdal and Rogaland. The Telemark rosemalers painted freely without the use of patterns. The colours are overlaid but allow the background to show through. Scrolls are outlined with long, flowing brush strokes. Examples of Telemark rosemaling can be seen in Oslo's Folk Museum, where log homes from the Telemark area have been relocated. The people from Telemark extended their craft to painting everything within their homes using mainly greys, blues and browns.

Hallingdal and Rogaland styles are very similar. Here the designs are symmetrical, but Hallingdal favours an orange/red/rust background, as used in Project 16. Rogaland is noted for its brilliant colour blending and intricate detail. Both styles use bold colours for their scrolling and flower motifs and more definite outlining than the freehand Telemark style.

Rosemaling began to decline in popularity as industrialization spread throughout Europe, producing a subsequent demand for mass-produced articles and materials. Although Norway, as a seafaring nation, incorporated decorative styles from the mainstream of European art, it also created its own distinctively Scandinavian art form.

HOLLAND: HINDELOOPER

In the seventeenth century the Dutch were the leading commercial power in Europe. As a seafaring nation Holland traded with many Far Eastern countries, such as Japan, China, Indonesia and India. Like their Scandinavian neighbours the Dutch were fascinated by the colourful exotic art of the East. During the winter months sailors painted objects in their homes to pass the time and to brighten their surroundings, incorporating the images of the Orient into their designs.

Stool decorated in the Telemark rosemaling style; jug painted in the Hindelooper manner

Hindeloopen, a town in northern Holland that was formerly one of the most important sea harbours, is famous for its folk painting, a tradition that has lasted for centuries. Until about the middle of the nineteenth century, the Hindeloopen inhabitants painted purely for themselves, the wealthier classes hiring professionals. The doors of pine cupboards and beds were painted to disguise the inferior wood of which they were made, as were cabinets, tables and all kinds of smaller household objects. Background colours were striking: red was popular, also blue, green and white. Created with fine brush work, acanthus leaf scrolls and flowers, with leaves and buds, were favourite motifs for the basic design. Scenes from the Bible, landscapes, birds and animals, both real and mythological, were often central to the design and encircled by vines and tendrils. Hindelooper painting is characterized by the colours and simple motifs, with line work and scrolls. I have painted a pair of clogs in the Hindelooper style showing birds and flowers as can be seen in Project 12.

When Hindeloopen's prosperity as a harbour declined, the townspeople realized that they could export their painting talents. One result of this was that the Norwegians brought wooden objects to be decorated in Holland, although the countries each developed their own completely different folk art styles. Hand-painted wall panels and doors were popular at the end of the eighteenth century, the artists copying the designs of the wood carvings of old masters. Hindeloopen is now famous for its fine furniture, which is derived from these old panel paintings.

RUSSIA: FOLK ART

Decorative folk art in Russia has an extremely long history. In the Ukraine, wall paintings can be traced back to the fourteenth century. The outside walls of houses were painted sparingly, with simple designs, but the interiors were lavishly decorated. Around the farms could be found sleds, beehives and carts adorned with beautifully painted decoration.

Flowers, leaves, fruit, birds and animals appeared on chests, plates and shutters. In the pagan world the motif of a bird perched on a branch functioned as a protector of hearth, home and peace. In the Christian world it represents joy, fulfilment and fertility. The traditional symbol of the Holy Trinity is expressed by a group of three flowers which, with the addition of buds, leaves and berries, are representative of love, charity and wisdom.

Russian flower painting is renowned for its boldness of design and colour. In the Moscow area flowers were painted in a realistic and quite distinctive style. The first japanned trays were made in the Urals in the early eighteenth century. Traditionally the trays were black brightened with bold flower patterns and enhanced with a painted gold border.

Red, black and gold are favoured colours in Russian folk painting, a fact which distinguishes this form from its European equivalent. In the village of Khokhloma a technique was perfected to highlight designs with metallic gold. Wooden objects, such as bowls, dishes and spoons, were painted with silver or aluminium, then varnished and tempered to an amber gold colour which characterizes this method of decoration. The traditional colours of black, red and gold with a gold border are used on the flat iron in Project 4.

The art of painting on papier-mâché was pioneered by peasant workers in the village of Fedoskino, near Moscow. Lacquered papier-mâché snuff boxes, chests and trays were first made in the early nineteenth century, using a method perfected by the English. The motif of a double eagle within an oval was the recognised trademark of a successful factory run by the Lukutin family in that area.

UNITED KINGDOM: NARROW BOAT PAINTING

A form of decorative folk art which can still be seen today is the characteristic decoration of the traditional canal narrow boats of the United Kingdom. Canals were first built in the eighteenth century, but at that time carrier boats were largely unpainted. In the middle of the nineteenth century bargees took their families to live on the boats and a period of distinctive and colourful decoration began. The origin of canal boat painting is still a matter for speculation, but it is probable that the cramped living conditions, coupled with the lack of possessions, motivated families to decorate their homes. Skilled dockyard painters became much in demand once the tradition had become established. As different dockyards developed, so individual dockyard painters each created their own style of rose painting as their personal hallmark.

The cabin doors of the narrow boats were a favourite place to display castles-and-roses designs. The simple dog

Buckby can, an example of the narrow boat painting style

rose that grows wild in the hedgerows along the canal banks could have been an inspiration for the stylized roses commonly painted. Similarly the castles and large country houses glimpsed in the distance could have inspired the painting of romantic castles. It is more likely, however, that the artists were following the prevailing popular taste: castles and roses were frequently painted on clock faces, trays and glass ware in the eighteenth century. The outside decoration of a boat was paid for by the owner, but the interior was the responsibility of the operating bargee. The tiny cabins were adorned with brilliant colours on every conceivable piece of furniture and every object. Enamel paint was used for the traditionally coloured red, yellow and white roses which were painted in groups.

The necessary implements of the boatman's trade, such as watering cans, jugs and mops, were kept outside on the cabin roof. These essential items were also liberally decorated, usually with vibrant colours on a black background. A common design on mop handles and steering arms was the barber's pole stripe in various colours. The decorated red jug in Project 3 is an example of roses used in narrow boat decoration.

Many of the narrow boats on canals in the UK today still display hand-painted roses, but unfortunately others are adorned with transfers, a poor imitation of the original hand-painted decoration. There are, however, boatyards and museums where this folk art can be seen and appreciated.

MODERN TECHNIQUES

While keeping to all these various traditions, modern artists are fortunate in having available so many new colours and techniques that it is now possible to bring a new and exciting richness to the designs of the past.

An example of a design using basic comma brush strokes occurs in Project 1, which shows the traditional approach.

Again, using mainly traditional brush strokes, I have painted the small watering can in Project 7 to bring spring to life, with the flowers of the English countryside, primroses, bluebells and daisies. Here the dipped crescent stroke is also demonstrated, to show how new brush materials can enhance the painting.

Two further crescent brush techniques are shown in Projects 17 and 19. I have used the pointed crescent brush stroke for the clematis petal in Project 17 against a sponged background. The jagged crescent brush stroke has been used to create a carnation in Project 19.

Ruffled crescent strokes on the sweet pea flowers in Project 14 also add interest to more traditional brush methods and here the delicate sweet pea pattern lends itself beautifully to the introduction of modern, soft, warm purples and pinks.

Twentieth-century paints allow the use of more vibrant colours too, such as the orange in the nasturtium design in Project 8, while yet keeping to traditional brush strokes.

Modern brushes provide the flexibility to work new designs, enabling the creation of perfect petals and leaves with one stroke, such as the elongated pointed crescent and jagged crescent brush strokes. Contemporary materials can also be utilized to enrich the surface of an article before decoration. Artificial sponges are a welcome invention, as is plastic foodwrap which can be used for a fake marbling effect. Advances in paint manufacture have given decorative painters not only a vast new range of colours but the opportunity of creating their own shades too. The improved quality of brushes allows the painting of more flowing and finer lines and complex detail.

CHAPTER 2

Equipment

All the equipment required for the projects in this book can usually be purchased from art and craft stores. Apart from brushes and paints, described in detail below, you will need a few miscellaneous supplies to enable you to start decorative painting. When painting with acrylics, you will need a wet palette (see Chapter 5 for details). A roll of kitchen paper, a jam jar, a synthetic sponge and tweezers are also required. Treated (coated) acetate is needed for practising brush strokes, plus masking tape to secure it to the pattern. Chapter 3 contains details of some materials required for the preparation of surfaces prior to actual decoration.

BRUSHES

The most important tools for the decorative folk artist are good brushes. Good-quality synthetic brushes are recommended; these are inexpensive, soft, tough and durable.

I have used the brushes listed in the table on page 16 to carry out all the project work. As brush sizes and refer-

FIG. 8

ence codes vary with different manufacturers, you will need to compare the ones you can obtain directly with those I have used. By matching brushes to the actual-size brush chart (see Fig. 8), you can ensure that you are using the right ones. It is useful if you mark any brush you match in this way with the reference code given in the brush table (page 16), so that you do not get confused later when reading the project painting instructions. A strip of masking tape wrapped around the end of the handle makes a suitable label for this purpose.

Brush identification

See Fig. 8.

Dalon D Series, produced by Daler-Rowney
- These all bear a 'D' prefix followed by a number code which describes the style of brush.
- The size is shown by a number code.

Prolene, produced by Pro Arte
- These are numerically coded to describe the brush style.
- The sizes are in imperial measurement and not coded.

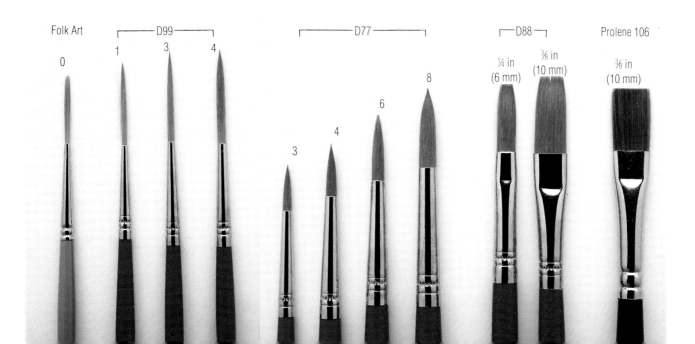

Folk Art — 0 · D99 — 1, 3, 4 · D77 — 3, 4, 6, 8 · D88 — ¼ in (6 mm), ⅜ in (10 mm) · Prolene 106 — ⅜ in (10 mm)

Folk Art, produced by Plaid Enterprises Inc.
- These are number referenced which gives the style.
- The size is shown by a number code.

Brush types and sizes

Name/ Style code	Size	Brush description
Dalon D77	Nos 3, 4, 6, 8	Round
Dalon D88	¼ in (6 mm) and ⅜ in (10 mm)	Square-edged
Prolene 106	⅜ in (10 mm)	Square-edged
Dalon D99	Nos 1, 3 and 4	Rigger or liner
Folk Art 40209	No. 0	Script liner

Which brush for which purpose?

The longer the brush hairs, the more paint the brush will hold and, therefore, the longer brush strokes can be.
- **The long, flat D88 ⅜-in (10-mm) brush** is ideal for undercoating, double and triple loading, floating colour and large comma and scroll work. An excellent brush for the majority of the crescent strokes; very versatile.
- **The shorter, flat, Prolene 106 ⅜-in (10-mm)** brush is ideal for undercoating, double loading, triple loading and floating colour and short comma strokes.
- **The D88 ¼-in (6-mm) brush** works well for double and triple loading and comma strokes. Not wide enough for most undercoating. Can be used for small crescent strokes.
- **The round brush D77, Nos 3, 4, 6 and 8**, is used mainly for flower petals, leaves, small scrolls and embellishments.
- **The rigger or liner brush D99, Nos 1, 3 and 4**, is used when longer strokes are required, including petals, leaves, scrolls and embellishments.
- **The Folk Art liner brush, No. 0**, is used whenever the line work needs to be fine and flowing, and also for scrolls and cross-hatching.

You will notice that I have included two flat brushes, both ⅜ in (10 mm) in size. When comparing these, you will see that one has shorter hairs. This brush is less flexible than the longer-haired one but moves well for certain flower petals when less flexibility is required, such as the rose petals in Project 18 and the carnation petals in Project 19.

I prefer to use the long-haired, more flexible brush for all strokes requiring a flat brush, but it is possible to use either brush if you cannot obtain both the recommended ⅜-in (10-mm) ones.

The parts of a brush

Brushes are comprised of three areas: brush hairs, ferrule and handle. The round brush also has a tip, whereas the flat brush comprises a chisel edge, knife edge and flat side (see Fig. 9). It is necessary to know these terms as they will be used to describe the movement of the brush: for example, 'Start on the chisel edge and add pressure on the flat . . .'

PAINTS

Both acrylic and oil paint can be used for decorative folk painting.

There are many manufacturers of free-flowing acrylic paint and a vast range of over 200 colours is produced. Many designs in decorative painting books require an endless list of acrylic colours, as the paints used are not mixed but taken directly from the bottle or tube. Purchasing all these colours in order that patterns can be followed is expensive, and finding the specified colour when required becomes an ordeal. In fact, knowing and finding what to use is confusing for the beginner.

A good supply of basic colours in oils or free-flowing acrylics is sufficient for any decorative painter. Experimenting with mixing your own colours is fun and you will create new colours when you least expect to! Using colours that you have mixed will make your design an original. I have used only four main colours on the milk can in Project 11; all the other colours were mixed.

For all decorative painting and various background techniques in this book I have used Cryla Flow acrylic paint made by Daler-Rowney, which has excellent flowing qualities. It comes in a range of good basic colours including metallics, yet an extensive range of both vibrant and pastel shades can be mixed. This paint covers exceptionally well and has the advantage of drying quickly. Cryla Flow is highly water-resistant when dry, allowing overpainting with no risk of smudging. The paint can also be applied to some flexible surfaces, such as treated acetate, without cracking or becoming brittle with age.

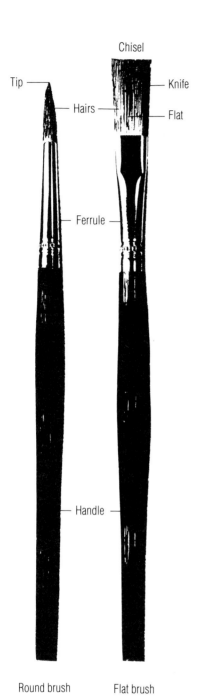

Chisel

Tip — — Knife

— Hairs — — Flat

— Ferrule —

— Handle —

Round brush   Flat brush

FIG. 9

Cryla Flow is similar in consistency to English double cream (North American heavy cream). This is a fraction thicker than water-based acrylic paints specifically manufactured for decorative painting, whose consistency is similar to that of soured cream. Both consistencies permit good brush strokes; however, do not use acrylic paints which are thicker than the consistency of English double cream without increasing the flow properties. See the section on acrylics in Chapter 5 for information on this technique.

I have included a Daler-Rowney tint chart (see page 141) to enable you to match the colours I have used with your own brand of acrylic or oil paints. Find what suits you best or, like me, stay with your favourite for the projects in this book.

When working with oils, it is important to read the section 'Oils' in Chapter 5 before starting any of the projects.

$\mathcal{P}$reparation of surfaces

If you are going to take the time to decorate an object, you should not begrudge the time required to prepare the surface. It is important that you wear protective clothing: rubber gloves, overalls and, where appropriate, a face mask.

You will require the following miscellaneous items:

- **Tack cloth** A sticky cloth which picks up particles of dust. If you cannot obtain this, always dust well with an ordinary, clean, soft cloth.
- **Grey wet-and-dry abrasive paper** Fine (600) and coarse. The lower the number, the coarser the paper.
- **Detergent** For cleaning metal ware.
- **Soft synthetic brushes** For varnishing, as bristle brushes can leave brush marks.
- **Paint brushes** Size according to the surface area to be painted.
- **White spirit** To clean brushes when oil-based products have been used.

PAINTS AND VARNISHES

For surface preparation it is advisable to use water-based products when intending to paint with acrylics and oil-based products when intending to paint with oils. There are on the market many paints and varnishes suitable for surface preparation and these can be purchased from large hardware and do-it-yourself stores. Decorative water-based paints, sold in traditional colours and specifically intended for small surfaces, can be purchased in bottles from craft stores.

A few words of caution are necessary regarding aerosol paints. A number of aerosol paints are available which are suitable for decorative work, and you need to be aware of the solvents used in them and what precautions need to be taken when handling these products, which can be harmful. Always read the manufacturer's instructions before attempting to spray.

For decorative painting, a smooth, blemish-free surface is the ideal. To allow good brush strokes a surface has to 'feel' right – like silk. To this end many surfaces require a coat of varnish *before* decorative painting begins. These include matt-finished surfaces already painted with oil- or water- based paints; natural wood and stained wood. There are, however, surfaces which *do not* require varnishing and you can trace your pattern straight on to these. They include surfaces created by the use of: satin- and silk-finish water- and oil-based paints; satin- and silk-finish water- and oil-based varnishes; coloured rust inhibitors; oil-based paints and sprays.

General information on varnish

Listed below are some tips on the suitability of varnishes. Obviously the choice of varnish will be dictated by the amount of wear and tear a decorated surface is expected to receive. For the majority of projects in this book I have found water-based varnish to be perfectly adequate. If you are antiquing, you will require oil-based varnish.

Bear in mind the following when choosing a varnish:

- For proof against medium heat (so as to withstand a hot coffee mug) and reasonable wear and tear, use an acrylic water-based varnish. This varnish has the advantage of being low-odour and quick-drying.
- For proof against greater heat and harder wear and tear, use a polyurethane varnish.
- For outdoor use (such as for house signs and mail boxes) where durability and flexibility are required, use an exterior varnish.
- For oil-based decoration, use an oil-based varnish: there can be an adverse reaction if a water-based varnish is used. Note that oil-based varnishes can slightly change the colour of your work, giving it a yellow tinge resembling an antiqued look.

Some acrylic varnishes have a milk-like appearance in the tin, but they do dry clear. Don't be tempted to apply this type of varnish too thickly: it is best spread quickly and evenly in two thin coats using a soft synthetic or foam brush. When varnishing natural wood, follow the grain of the wood. Always remember to stir varnish thoroughly before use and never apply it to a surface which has not thoroughly dried.

Varnishing is best carried out in a warm, dust-free environment. Do not place varnished work in strong sunlight, nor near fires, radiators or stoves. Keep a special brush for varnishing and clean it well at the end of each session. Replace lids on varnish tins as soon as possible.

Varnishes come in three different finishes: matt, satin and gloss. I prefer the satin finish for decorative painting as this has slightly more sheen than the matt finish but less than the gloss. As with gloss paint, the surface created by the gloss varnish is too shiny and therefore feels slippery when brush strokes are applied. When using gloss varnish, sand with wet-and-dry a little more thoroughly before painting.

Drying time varies with different varnishes. Some will be touch-dry within hours, but some may not reach their maximum strength for up to two weeks. Always be guided by the manufacturer's instructions when following the procedures set out below for the preparation of wood and metal.

Never use a coloured varnish. Always use the same varnish throughout the preparation and finishing of a piece of work. Failure to keep to the same varnish can result in a crackle effect.

PREPARATION OF WOOD
....

Preparing a painted surface from bare wood

Decorative painting on wood with an oily, open-grain surface, such as teak, is not recommended. It is best to choose a wood which does not require a wood filler to fill the grain, though you can use a type with the odd knot hole, for which you will need filler. I used pine wood for the spinner's chair in Project 5, for instance, and also for the stool in Project 9.

The procedure for preparing a painted surface from bare wood is outlined below:

1 Bare wood, even the best, always requires sanding and may need extensive work to smooth down those places where tools leave rough edges. Make sure that nails are well inset and holes are filled. When wood filler is required, purchase the natural shade and follow the manufacturer's instructions. Fill even the smallest holes.

2 For fine sanding I prefer grey wet-and-dry abrasive papers. Use 300 coarse paper for general-purpose work and finish sanding with a fine 600 or even higher-numbered paper. Cut the abrasive paper up into small pieces so that you can sand difficult corners. For large, flat surfaces use abrasive paper folded around a block of wood. When sanding, sand with the grain of the wood: for example, the inside of a bowl should be sanded around its contours.

3 After sanding, dust your wooden ware thoroughly with a tack cloth.

4 Seal the wood with a suitable primer. The back of your wooden ware should always be finished, as well as the front, because this makes the piece more attractive and also protects against warping.

5 Sand again and remove the dust with a tack cloth.

6 Paint one or two coats of finishing paint in the background colour following the manufacturer's instructions.

7 Sand again and remove the dust with a tack cloth.

8 Apply the final coat of varnish.

9 As a final preparation before decorating, wet-sand with the 600 wet-and-dry abrasive paper and wipe with a damp cloth.

Preparing a natural varnished surface from bare wood

1 Sand and dust as described in steps 1–3 above.

2 Seal the wood with a water-based wood stain, acrylic wash or wood sealer.

3 Sand and dust.

4 Apply one coat of varnish.

5 Sand and dust.

6 Apply the final coat of varnish.

7 Sand and dust as described in step 9 above.

Procedure for old painted wood

Project 13 contains an example of old painted wood: a chest of drawers which was already painted white. The

Wooden chest of drawers before preparation

old paint obviously had loose brush hairs and dust in it when it dried, which is often the case when care has not been taken in painting. However, in this instance the paint was sound, so it was not necessary to remove it all and sand down to the bare wood.

If old paint is fairly smooth and sound, the following procedure applies:

1 Sand the surface well, checking for any holes which may need filling.

2 Fill the holes with wood filler and sand these areas when dry.

3 Remove all dust thoroughly with a tack cloth.

4 Apply paint according to the manufacturer's instructions.

5 Follow steps 7, 8 and 9 of 'Preparing a painted surface from bare wood' (page 19).

If the paint is flaking or you want a natural wood grain finish, the following procedure applies:

1 Apply paint remover according to the manufacturer's instructions and scrape off all paint. Take great care with application and disposal of this chemical.

2 Sand the surface well with a medium abrasive paper

(300) until all traces of old paint have been removed and dust with a tack cloth.

3 Follow steps 1–7 of 'Preparing a natural varnished surface from bare wood' (page 19).

Preparing a painted surface from medium-density fibreboard

Medium-density fibreboard was used to make the paddle (Project 1), clock (Project 18), cheese platter (Project 16) and the shelf (Project 8) as it is easy to cut into shape. It also requires less preparation than natural wood. Acrylic base coats are particularly suitable for this surface.

To prepare medium-density fibreboard, proceed as follows:

1 Sand the surface lightly with 600 wet-and-dry abrasive paper and remove all dust thoroughly with a tack cloth

2 Follow steps 6–9 of 'Preparing a painted surface from bare wood' (page 19).

PREPARATION OF METAL

Preparing rusty articles

Metal ware offered for sale often looks too rusty and dirty even to consider buying. However, if the articles are sound, with no missing parts, rust and dirt can be dealt with.

1 Soak the article in hot water and liquid detergent to remove grease.

2 With a strong bristle brush or steel wool, clean off all loose particles. Rinse and dry.

3 Repeat steps 1 and 2 if not totally free of grease and rust particles.

4 Fill in any holes with plastic filler and rub down with coarse abrasive paper.

5 Sand the surface with 600 wet-and-dry abrasive paper. Remove dust with a tack cloth.

6 Apply an anti-rust primer to give extra corrosion resistance before applying a rust inhibitor. Rust inhibitors come in the form of paint in a tin or aerosol can.

Note: I have used coloured aerosol rust inhibitors in some of the projects, including the enamel jug in Project 3.

Oval metal fish pan before preparation

7 Lightly sand with 600 wet-and-dry abrasive paper and remove dust with a tack cloth.

8 If necessary, apply a final coat using varnish and lightly sand and dust before applying decoration.

Preparing a surface on non-rusty articles

1 Repeat steps 1–5 of 'Preparing rusty articles' (page 20).

2 Apply the appropriate primer following the manufacturer's instructions: for example, use etching primer for galvanized metals.

3 Paint one or two undercoat(s).

4 Lightly sand with 600 wet-and-dry abrasive paper and remove dust with a tack cloth.

5 Apply the finishing coat of paint and lightly sand and dust.

6 If necessary, apply a final coat using varnish and lightly sand and dust before applying decoration.

Preparing new tin ware

1 Wash in warm, soapy water to remove any oily film, rinse and dry well. Use a hair dryer to remove moisture from rolled seams.

2 Rub the surface with very fine steel wool to remove the shine. Be careful not to scratch through the tin plating.

3 Repeat steps 6–8 of 'Preparing rusty articles' (pages 20–1).

General note: Occasionally, during painting of a design, 'peeling' can occur whereby the acrylic paint and the prepared surface seem to part. A little more wet sanding of the surface will help prevent this.

CHAPTER 4

Plain and decorative backgrounds

•••••••••••••••••••••

Most decorative folk art is painted on a plain back ground. However, experimenting with different background techniques, ranging from traditional antique to 3-D marbling, can give the final painting a unique look.

CHOOSING THE RIGHT BACKGROUND
••

You can use the background specified for each project, or choose a different one, as shown in the colour illustration. Here are some guidelines to help you select the right colour for a background, which will make all the difference to your finished project. A paint dispenser colour chart will prove a useful aid. For an authentic look it is advisable to keep to traditional colours for, say, milk churns, watering cans and frying pans – that is, antique green, brown earth colours, black and slate blue.

Black is a good background colour for the beginner as practically every shade of paint, apart from the very darkest, can be painted on to a black background. It is ideal for vibrant-coloured designs, such as poppies, nasturtiums and Russian and English canal ware styles.

Similarly cream, which is a pastel shade in itself, can be used as a background colour without the worry of wondering whether colours will tone well. Cream is used for the waste-paper bin in Project 2. Pure white backgrounds are not normally successful.

Many shades of green and blue can be used successfully for most projects, as these provide a natural look. The background for the fuchsia pattern on the chest of drawers in Project 13 is a dark pine green, giving a natural effect.

The bright-coloured roses of English canal ware are usually seen on black backgrounds, but they look equally good on bright greens, blues and reds, as shown by the red jug in Project 3.

Remember that if you do not like the colour of the background you have created, you have only one option – repaint it! Never paint on a background you are unhappy with, as you will not be doing your painting justice.

Before attempting the following background techniques ask yourself these three questions:

1 Has my design small flowers and embellishments? If the answer is 'Yes', avoid the textured techniques created with plastic foodwrap, sponging or reverse stencilling, as these are too busy and will detract from the final decoration. Keep the background plain.

2 Is the item to be painted traditional? If the answer is 'Yes', keep to a plain background. A marbled background may work well on a clock, but not on a milk churn!

3 Is my background natural wood? If the answer is 'Yes', no more texture is needed as wood has all the texture necessary for an attractive background.

All the background techniques used in the projects are described in detail. It is a good idea to practise them on wood or card, as appropriate, and keep them as trial cards for use under your painted acetates.

ACRYLIC WASH
••••••••••••••••••••

Acrylic wash has been used on the spinner's chair in Project 5. Wooden items with attractive graining can be enhanced by this method, which is suitable only for bare wood.

Procedure for acrylic wash

1 Dilute acrylic paint with water, making sure that there is sufficient wash to cover the whole of the surface. Use the appropriate-sized container for mixing water with paint and mix well with a spatula. (Never use brush hairs for mixing.)

2 Use a large synthetic or sponge brush and paint the surface with acrylic wash. Avoid soaking the surface as this causes warping of the wood.

3 Allow to dry well and sand before applying two coats of varnish.

SPRAYED BORDERS
••••••••••••

This technique is used in two different ways in this book. On the wooden tray in Project 10, where the expanse of green was harsh and needed to be softened, a gold edging was added to give a touch of elegance to the finished decoration. In Project 7 the round watering can, used for the spring flower design, was painted pale blue and then sprayed a slightly darker shade of blue around the circumference, which resulted in an interesting but unobtrusive background.

Watering can (Project 7) illustrating the use of the technique for sprayed borders; waste-paper bin (Project 2) showing the use of spattering (see page 24)

Procedure for sprayed borders

1 Prepare and paint the surface.

2 Place the surface to be sprayed in an upright position, thus avoiding spraying directly down on to it. It is useful to have a turntable so that the object can be moved during spraying.

3 Hold the aerosol can with the contrasting colour at least 30 cm (12 in) away from the surface to be sprayed. Depress the nozzle, making sure that the first spray of paint is aimed slightly to the side of the surface, as the initial jet is usually concentrated. Move the aerosol can so that the spray falls lightly on the areas which will be decorated.

Note: Should you wish to avoid aerosols, edges can be spattered instead (see page 24). The effect will not be quite such a fine, even spray.

REVERSE STENCILLING
••••••••••••••••••••••••••••••

Reverse stencilling is a simple method of designing a background, only effective if the final decoration is simple. The technique is used in Project 19, where a delicate, natural background of ferns behind the carnations enhances the flowers.

If you are uncertain which colours to choose for stencilling, use light and dark shades of the same colour. You can experiment and have fun!

Make your own stencils by using, for example, leaves, lace, paper doilies or net curtaining – in fact, anything you can think of which could act as a stencil can be used. There are many attractive leaves in our gardens and countryside which make an ideal background for flowers using the reverse stencil technique.

Procedure for reverse stencilling

1 Prepare the surface and paint the base colour.

2 When the base colour is dry, place the stencil on top.

3 Add sufficient adhesive to the back of the stencil to hold it in position.

4 Spray or spatter (see right) the second colour over the stencil and allow to dry.

5 Remove the stencil to reveal an attractive, two-toned background.

6 Varnish and sand lightly before painting.

ANTIQUING BEFORE DECORATING

It is possible to antique the background of a design before painting. This can be achieved by adding colour to the varnish prior to decorating. The technique is used on the shelf in Project 8. The shelf had a cream base coat, so I used two colours, Yellow Ochre and Burnt Sienna for the antiquing effect. Other colours can be used for antiquing, depending on the background colour of the design and your personal preference. For Project 8 I used a water-based varnish with acrylic paint. For oil-based varnish, use oil paint.

Procedure for antiquing before decorating

1 Prepare and paint the surface.

2 Varnish the object and allow to dry.

3 Use a flat 1-in (25-mm) synthetic brush loaded with varnish and wipe the edge of the brush through the first colour (Yellow Ochre in the case of Project 8), also picking up a little of the second colour (Burnt Sienna). Brush along the edges and corners of the object with long brush strokes,

working quickly to avoid the varnish drying before the antiquing is in place.

4 Allow to dry, sand lightly and the surface is ready for decoration.

SPATTERING

Used on its own with one colour or several, or combined with other techniques, spattering is attractive. The technique involves simply flicking paint from a bristle brush on to a background colour to give a flecked effect. Spattering was used on the cream base coat of the waste-paper bin in Project 2.

Subtle effects can be achieved when the spattered paint is in lighter or darker tones, or both, than the main background colour. Spattering produces an excellent background for decorative folk painting as it is unobtrusive, covers slight blemishes in the background paint (should you have any!) and is fun to do. A few words of warning before attempting to spatter: the paint can go where least expected, so cover up surrounding surfaces, as well as yourself!

Examples of (left to right) spattering, imprinting with plastic foodwrap and fake marbling with plastic foodwrap.

Procedure for spattering

1 Prepare and paint the surface.

2 Dilute the acrylic paint with sufficient water for the area to be spattered.

3 Touch the diluted paint with a stencil brush or toothbrush so as to cover just the tip of the bristles and lightly touch the bristles on to a piece of kitchen paper to remove excess paint.

4 Drag your thumb across the bristles so that the paint spatters in the direction of the surface to be spattered. Try spattering the edges more to give a denser distribution in that area.

5 If spattering with more than one colour, wait until the first colour has dried, then repeat steps 2–4.

6 Varnish the surface and sand lightly before applying decoration.

Note: For smaller surfaces a finer spatter can be achieved by using a small, short-haired paintbrush. Hold the brush over the surface with one hand and 'tickle' the hairs with the forefinger of the other.

FAKE MARBLING
· · · · · · · · · · · · · · · · · · · ·

Fake marbling is achieved by painting a surface with a base coat, allowing it to dry and then painting a different colour on top; while this colour is still wet, plastic foodwrap is used to lift off some of the paint. The paint that remains creates the fake marbled effect.

I used this technique with two colours for the soft background to the clock in Project 18 as the rose design is simple without embellishments and fake marbling is decorative in itself.

Procedure for fake marbling

1 Prepare the surface and apply the base coat.

2 Tear off a piece of plastic foodwrap from the roll: it should be at least 15 cm (6 in) longer than the painted surface. *Do not* economize when using plastic foodwrap.

3 Add retarder (see page 27) to a piece of kitchen paper and wipe a thin layer of retarder over the surface to be marbled.

4 Dilute the chosen colour of acrylic paint with sufficient water to paint the whole surface, remembering that a highly diluted paint creates a soft effect and a thicker paint produces a heavier texture.

5 Paint the whole surface using a flat synthetic or sponge brush, working quickly at this stage.

6 Hold the plastic foodwrap by the top two corners so that it hangs down and slowly allow it to fall *loosely* on to the wet paint so that creases are formed in the plastic and the whole area is covered.

7 Use your fingers to push the plastic into more creases to form different abstract shapes, ensuring that the surface edges are not forgotten.

8 Carefully remove the plastic foodwrap by lifting two corners.

9 Allow the surface to dry thoroughly before varnishing and sand lightly before applying the decoration.

Note: When the paint is dry, steps 3–8 can be repeated with another colour for a multi-coloured fake marble. In this case it is advisable to use very thin paint.

IMPRINTS
· · · · · · · · · · · · · ·

The effect of imprints with plastic foodwrap is similar to fake marbling but the texture is denser.

Procedure for imprints

1 Prepare the surface and apply the base coat.

2 Crumple small pieces of plastic foodwrap into balls.

3 Add a little retarder to a piece of kitchen paper and wipe the surface to be decorated.

4 Dilute the acrylic paint with sufficient water to cover the surface area. (If you wish, you can apply two colours instead of one.)

5 Working quickly at this stage, paint the whole surface with one or two colours using a flat synthetic or sponge brush.

6 Press the plastic into the wet paint, turning it, and replace when full of paint. This process will lift the paint from the surface and reveal abstract shapes.

7 Allow to dry thoroughly before varnishing and lightly sanding, ready for decorating.

Note: Kitchen paper and even leaves can be used for making imprints. Lay them flat on the wet surface and then remove them.

SPONGING
••••••••••••••••

You can create more varied effects with sponging than with any other decorative technique, yet it is the simplest. The table shown in the photograph on page 123 was sponged using the method for small surfaces described below.

Any type of sponge can be used, each type resulting in a different-textured effect. The cellulose sponge will give the large hole effect, the natural sponge slightly smaller holes, and foam, on the whole, a denser texture. It is worthwhile purchasing different-textured sponges and experimenting.

The sponge can be used to dab on colour or pressed into wet paint to remove colour. I use water-based paints for all sponging.

Creative effects can be achieved by loading a sponge with two colours at once. One colour can be sponged over another when the first coat is dry, for a crisp impression or, when it is wet, for a cloudier look. The sponge prints may be heavy or delicate depending on the pressure applied. Try moving the sponge in different directions, while dabbing, to achieve different patterns: for instance, diagonally, horizontally, vertically or round the edges of circular objects.

Procedure for sponging large areas

This procedure is suitable for large objects, such as chests of drawers, and walls.

1 Paint the prepared surface with a base coat and allow to dry.

2 Pour paint into a shallow tray.

3 Moisten a sponge (about the size of your hand) with water.

4 Dip the dampened sponge lightly into the paint. Dab off excess paint on a piece of kitchen paper.

5 Press several imprints on to the surface. Work diagonally for a more interesting design.

6 Repeat steps 4 and 5 until all the surface is sponged.

7 Do not varnish walls. For furniture, allow to dry thoroughly and then varnish ready for decorative painting.

Procedure for sponging small surfaces

This procedure is suitable for small areas, such as the table in Project 17.

1 Paint the prepared surface with a base coat and allow to dry.

2 Add retarder to a piece of kitchen paper and wipe a thin layer of retarder over the surface to be sponged.

3 Dilute acrylic paint with sufficient water to sponge the surface area.

4 Dip small pieces (approximately 5cm (2in) in diameter) of dry sponge into one or two colours as desired, dabbing off excess paint when necessary.

5 Press several imprints on to the surface, then reload. Work diagonally for a more interesting design.

6 Repeat steps 4 and 5 until all the surface is sponged.

7 When the surface is thoroughly dry, varnish it ready for decorative painting.

Note: Always remember to finish the edges.

Problem solving

☛ **Repetition of pattern** Change the sponge and direction more often.
☛ **Pattern too heavy: needs more background showing through** Use less paint. To solve the problem, 'reverse' the process by dipping the sponge into the base-coat paint and press imprints on to the surface.

CHAPTER 5

Painting with acrylics and oils

....

ACRYLICS

....

Even without previous painting experience, you will find acrylics easy and a pleasure to use. As mentioned earlier, acrylics are water-based, dry quickly and clean up easily when wet. They also dry to a flexible, plastic and durable finish much more rapidly than oils and eliminate the hazards associated with the solvents used when painting with oil-based paints.

The drying time will vary depending upon air humidity and temperature. It is important with all acrylic paints used for decorative painting to allow sufficient time for any undercoat to dry before applying the top decoration, and for this reason it is always useful to keep a hair dryer by your side.

Read the manufacturer's instructions for your particular brand of paint before trying the various mediums available which control the paint. Generally speaking, it is advisable to use mediums from the same manufacturer as your paints. You may find the following mediums useful:

- **Water tension breaker (or flow medium)** Reduces brush marks. Ideal for floating colour, overstrokes, tendrils and scrolls.
- **Glaze medium** Increases the drying time of acrylics. The slightly thicker nature of the medium gives an added depth to the final glaze.
- **Retarder** Comes in liquid or gel form. Helps slow the drying time of acrylic paint. Can marginally add to the transparency of the colour – essential for keeping paint wet while blending.
- **Water** Those of you who have painted with acrylics for many years may find that the only medium with which you are comfortable is water. Good! But please be careful not to dilute the colour too much as 'peeling' from the surface can then occur.

Dos and don'ts of painting with acrylics

- Do make or purchase a wet palette.
- Do wear protective clothing, such as an old shirt with sleeves, as acrylic paint is difficult to remove once it has dried.
- Do take good care of your brushes.
- Don't put the brush hairs in your mouth to reshape the brush!

Care of acrylic brushes

Unless brushes are given proper care, they will be spoiled and lose their shape. Follow these simple rules:

- When painting, always lay the brushes flat so that only the brush hairs are in water.
- To clean brushes use cold water for removing the acrylic paint, followed by household soap worked to a lather on the palm of the hand. Use your thumb nail to push paint from the ferrule area out of the brush hairs. Repeat until there is no trace of colour. Rinse and reshape the brush. Always stand upright on the handle end and allow to dry.
- If brushes are to be stored for any length of time, make sure that they are thoroughly clean and dry beforehand.
- Should brushes become clogged and stiff with paint, use a brush cleaner specifically for acrylic paints and follow the manufacturer's instructions.
- Never use acrylic brushes for oil paint or *vice versa*.
- Never 'make do' with a brush that is past its best – your painting deserves better, so treat yourself to a new one! Remember: good painting needs good brushes.

Use of retarder with acrylic paint

As already mentioned, a retarder medium is used to prolong the drying time of acrylics. It can be mixed directly into the paint on the palette or brushed on to the base coat or undercoat before the decorative coat of paint.

When painting the fruit in Projects 9 and 10, I used retarder to allow more time for blending. I also use retarder when dry brushing the centre of daisies, as in Project 5. A longer drying time is needed for various background techniques, such as sponging and marbling, too.

When using retarder, follow the manufacturer's instructions; as a general rule, however, only a few drops of retarder are required when mixed into a puddle of paint. It is advisable to use as little retarder as possible when painting, because it will marginally increase the transparency of the paint.

The drying time will depend on the climatic conditions and the amount of retarder used in the paint. Before varnishing it is advisable to give the painting extra time to dry or, alternatively, use a hair dryer to hasten the drying process. If the surface is varnished before the retarder has completely dried, the varnish, in the area where the retarder was used, will feel sticky and remain that way for a very long time.

Removal of acrylic paint from fabric

Because of the high pigment content of acrylic paint – necessary to produce bright colours – complete removal of this paint from fabric is often impossible. Protective clothing is therefore recommended. Should you need to clean any spillage from fabric, proceed as follows. If the paint is still wet, pad the back of the fabric and rub the paint with a wet cloth. It is important to pad the back of the fabric to avoid spreading the stain. If the paint has dried, you may be able to remove it by scratching the surface.

How a wet palette works

Acrylic colours dry by evaporation, so moisture is required to keep the paints workable. The wet palette replaces the moisture lost by evaporation. It is worth noting that as certain acrylic paints used for decorative painting have a higher water content than others, a strip palette rather than a wet palette is sometimes recommended for these. A polystyrene meat tray will also suffice. Check the paint manufacturer's instructions before purchasing a wet palette.

There are various wet palettes on the market, but basically the principle is the same. It is possible to make your own, which will do the job just as well. It is important to use a *shallow* container of approximately the same size as a wet palette refill. This will give you sufficient space for blending on the palette. Preferably choose a container with a loose-fitting lid, although you can use plastic food-wrap. You will also need a small, shallow tray for the brushes, such as the lid from a plastic margarine container.

If you intend to paint regularly with acrylics, I recommend purchasing a wet palette. The standard wet palette consists of a tray divided into two areas, one for the brush and the other for the paint. When not in use, the palette, with the paint, can be covered with the lid. Replacing the lid will reduce evaporation and leave the acrylic colours moist and workable for days – even weeks.

While you are working, the paint is kept moist by being placed on two pieces of paper in the paint area of the wet palette. The bottom piece, which is thick and absorbent and similar to blotting paper, is called reservoir paper. The top piece, which is thin, is known as membrane paper: moisture passes through it from the reservoir paper into the paint. This allows you to work all day with the paint uncovered, although it may be necessary to dampen the reservoir paper occasionally.

Preparing a wet palette

1 Place the reservoir paper in the bottom of the tray and add water to dampen (a spray can be useful for this purpose). Pour off any excess water. Check the reservoir paper for correct wetness by placing a piece of kitchen paper over the top to absorb any excess moisture. Remove the kitchen paper.

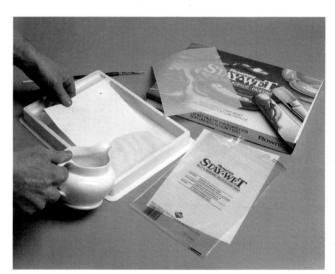

2 Place the membrane paper on top of the reservoir paper.

3 Fill the brush receptacle with sufficient water to cover the brush hairs *slightly* into the ferrule area.

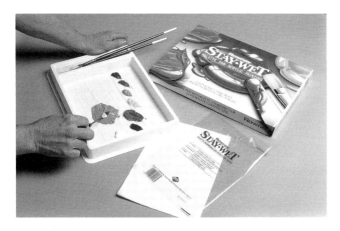

4 Squeeze your acrylic paint on to the wet palette, allowing sufficient in view of the fact that it will keep workable for days.

5 When you have finished using the wet palette, check the wetness of the reservoir paper and add more water if necessary. Throw away the water in the brush receptacle and wipe clean. Replace the lid.

Problem solving

- **Curling of membrane paper** This is usually caused by warm temperatures drying the reservoir paper quickly. Keep a spray handy to replace moisture in the reservoir paper to prevent the paint becoming dry.
- **Acrylic paint has a skin forming, becoming hard and 'bitty'** The reservoir paper has been allowed to dry. The remedy is to throw away the membrane and reservoir paper and start again.
- **Acrylic paint bleeding into other colours** The answer here is that the reservoir paper and membrane paper are far too wet. Discard the membrane paper, including all paint that is bleeding, and remove excess water from the reservoir paper with a piece of kitchen paper. Insert new membrane paper.
- **Mould growing in the wet palette** There is no real cure for this problem as certain climatic conditions and the dampness of the palette are ideal for promoting mould growth. Clean the wet palette thoroughly, wearing a pair of rubber gloves, and wipe it with household bleach. Rinse under cold, running water to remove all traces of bleach before setting up the palette again, this time using distilled water to inhibit mould.

Palette layout

If you are a beginner in decorative folk painting, it is helpful to start by learning the palette layout as this way you will learn to identify colours faster; you will also find it easier to tell dark colours apart, especially when painting under artificial light. Even when using two or three colours on your palette, it is always best to place them in the same position. The centre of the palette can be left free for any mixing. The palette layout shown in Fig. 10 (page 30) is similar to a colour wheel, with warm colours on one side and cool colours on the other.

OILS
....

While I am now converted to acrylics, I originally learnt decorative folk painting in Canada using oils. On returning to England I found my favourite oils unobtainable, so decided to change to acrylics. If you feel comfortable using oils and wish to use them for the projects in this book, you will find it helpful to read the following.

- Ensure that your brushes are suitable for oils and are of the correct size. It is possible to use the same brushes as recommended for acrylics, but their life span will be shorter because of the effects of the solvents used with oils.

FIG. 10

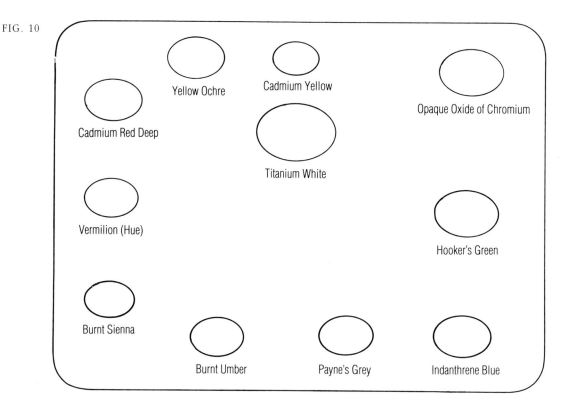

- Ensure that your brushes are suitable for oils and are of the correct size. It is possible to use the same brushes as recommended for acrylics, but their life span will be shorter because of the effects of the solvents used with oils.
- Oils take much longer to dry than acrylics. As a general rule, linseed oil added to oil paint will prolong the drying time, whereas white spirit will not.
- A drying medium is available to help speed the drying process. It can also assist to paint all the undercoating on several objects at once, otherwise time is wasted waiting for objects to dry each time. For example, Projects 8 and 15 require undercoating and both could be done simultaneously.
- Make sure that the consistency of the paint is like double cream. To help achieve this consistency add a medium consisting of equal parts linseed oil, white spirit and varnish.
- When using paint for line work, add more white spirit to thin it.
- For dots, add more medium to the paint to make it the consistency of single cream.
- Mix paint using a palette knife.
- Load the brush as described for acrylic paint (see Chapter 6).

- Wash the brush in white spirit and wipe lightly with a lint-free rag before loading.
- For the wet palette substitute a strip palette or a thin piece of wood with a non-porous surface.
- Omit the use of a retarder in all projects.
- Omit the use of a hair dryer (patience is a virtue!).
- In projects where floating colour is used, substitute white spirit for water and ensure that the undercoat is completely dry.
- When oil paint is not in use for a short period of time, cover with plastic foodwrap and place in a cool area. For longer periods, use a glass container with a metal (not plastic) lid for storing paint left over from the palette. Remove the paint from the palette with a palette knife and place it around the inside edge of the container. Fill the container half-full with water, replace the lid and turn upside down.
- To clean oil from brushes after use, rinse well in white spirit or low-odour thinner. Wipe dry and dip into baby oil. This helps brushes to remain soft and last longer. Remember to rinse brushes in white spirit before you next use them for painting.
- Always store brushes upright, never resting on their hairs.
- Allow paint to dry thoroughly before applying varnish.

CHAPTER 6

Basic brush strokes and pattern work

Decorative folk painting looks so professional that it is difficult to believe that designs are made up with basic brush strokes. The patterns are simple and the first basic brush stroke is a comma. The size of the stroke depends on the size of brush and the pressure on that brush. For larger flower heads, for example, do not struggle with a small brush but use the size suitable for the petal size required.

BEING IN CONTROL

When painting, always move the brush handle so that you are pulling the hairs towards you, then you are in control of the brush stroke. By pulling the brush away from you, you do not have the same control over the stroke.

Decorative folk painters need to move their arms when painting as this provides better control and freedom. For this reason always sit comfortably when painting. Sitting at a table or desk of normal height is detrimental to good brush strokes as the table will be too high. You will notice that you have to lift your arm up to work on the table. *For decorative painting you need to have your arm fully mobile*, not just your hand. To find the correct height at which you should work, sit on a chair and hold a tray on your lap.

Experiment with the following:

1 Sit at a regular-height table and hold a brush in your hand, as you would a pencil, while resting your wrist on the table. Now see how little movement you have when your wrist has to remain resting on the table and you can use only your fingers to control the movement of the brush.

2 Sit on a chair and place a tray on your lap. Take a brush in your hand and hold it at 80 degrees, slightly less than perpendicular. Use your little finger as a 'rest', leaving a 'finger size' gap between the little finger and the next finger. Your little finger will be used to help control the brush by acting as a pivot or an artist's rest.

The author showing the importance of a comfortable sitting position that allows free arm movement

Holding the brush correctly

Move the whole of your arm from the shoulder and, still using your little finger as a rest, move the brush around, making imaginary strokes. You will notice how much more freedom you have to make flowing brush strokes.

You will be painting objects of varying size, from flat trays to chests of drawers and milk churns. Make sure that the object is placed at the correct height so that you are in control. For example, a milk churn is best laid on its back wedged on a turntable for decorative painting. Drawers are best placed on end between your legs and raised up to the correct working height. Small tables are more complicated, but quite often they can straddle your legs. Move the objects around to the position where you feel most comfortable.

LOADING THE BRUSH

Never overload your brush with paint. Always load the paint approximately two-thirds of the way up the brush hairs towards the ferrule. Experience will show that the larger the brush head, the more paint required. Longer-haired flat brushes are often underloaded by the beginner, but practice makes perfect.

Procedure for loading

1 Immerse the brush hairs in water half-way up the ferrule and wipe the brush lightly across a piece of kitchen paper. Check the ferrule area to see if there are any water droplets, as these will slide down the brush and into the paint if they are not removed.

2 Hold the brush at a 45-degree angle and stroke the brush hairs, on both sides, through the edge of the puddle of paint, making strokes approximately 2.5–5 cm (1–2 in) in length on the wet palette. Load until the brush is loaded two-thirds of the way up the hairs towards the ferrule. *Never dip the brush directly down into the puddle of paint*, but always 'stroke' the paint on the palette. Note that a flat brush needs to be loaded by placing the flat sides down.

3 The paint on the wet palette should appear as in the photograph below when loading: that is, there should be an area of paint to one side which has been pulled by the brush.

Loading the brush

4 When loaded, the brush hairs should return to their original shape with *a smooth surface of paint and no blobs evident.*

BASIC BRUSH STROKES

On the following pages I will be explaining, with the aid of worksheets, how to paint the basic brush strokes for decorative folk painting. Trace the brush strokes with your brush. Do not be tempted to paint freehand at this stage as your brush strokes will lose their shape. Wait until you have painted Projects 1 and 2.

Do not be discouraged if at first you cannot paint the perfect brush stroke. Folk art has survived because people took the time to create beautiful brush strokes. As with any other pastime, whether it be aerobics or learning to play an instrument, you need to practise. Remember to be patient, to practise and be positive and know that you can do it. Keep practising until you feel happy with your brush strokes. Don't worry if you have had to attempt more than a hundred comma strokes before achieving a good one: it will be worth it.

When painting, strive for contrast in your brush strokes. It is natural for beginners to panic if they feel they have painted a brush stroke which they know to be poor. There is nothing you can do but leave it. It is important that you recognized this poor brush work and can try to perfect it next time. Repainting over the top will create a result worse than the original. It is far better to distract the eye from this area by painting good brush strokes elsewhere. Only you know you made a mistake; others will think that, because it is present, it was intentional.

Using the practice worksheets

1 Place a piece of coated acetate over the worksheet and secure lightly with masking tape. If you wish, you can photocopy the worksheet rather than working direct from the book; you may find this easier and the book runs less risk of being damaged.

2 Place the worksheet squarely in front of you, so that the comma stroke is directly in front of your painting hand and not to one side. (If you are left-handed, you may want to turn the worksheet a quarter-turn to the right, which helps if you paint from right to left.)

Note: When painting the border pattern at the bottom of the worksheet, because both comma and straight strokes are in the horizontal position, you will need to turn your worksheet round through 90 degrees and paint as before in the vertical position.

3 Load the brush indicated by the worksheet and refer again to the instructions on how to hold the brush in 'Being in control' (page 31) before tracing the brush strokes on the acetate.

4 *Reload the brush for each brush stroke.* There is no need to wash the brush when loading with the same colour.

Round brush strokes worksheet

Comma stroke

The comma is the first and most important brush stroke for the decorative folk artist and the most versatile. This is how you do it:

1 Place the brush just slightly below the top of the comma stroke on the worksheet and add pressure to spread the brush hairs.

2 Gradually pull the brush towards you, releasing the pressure by lifting the brush, until it is finally on its tip at the end of the stroke. Stop and lift the brush. Notice how the shape of your stroke depends entirely on pressure and release. Do not twist the brush.

Straight stroke

1 Place the brush slightly below the top of the brush stroke on the worksheet and add pressure to the brush to spread the hairs.

2 Gradually release pressure while pulling the brush towards you. At the same time slightly twist the brush by pushing your thumb forwards against it. Finally finish on the tip of the brush.

Note: If you have difficulty with lifting, pulling and twisting in step 2, leave out the twisting and add the twist when you have perfected the lifting and pulling.

'S' stroke

1 Keep the paint smooth all round the tip of the brush and start to paint a thin line, gradually increasing pressure in the first curve of the stroke and keeping that pressure until the brush comes out of the second curve.

2 Gradually release pressure, finishing on the tip of the brush.

'C' stroke

Keep the paint smooth all round the tip of the brush and paint a thin line. Slowly add pressure with the most pressure in the centre of the 'C', then slowly lift the brush, finishing on the tip.

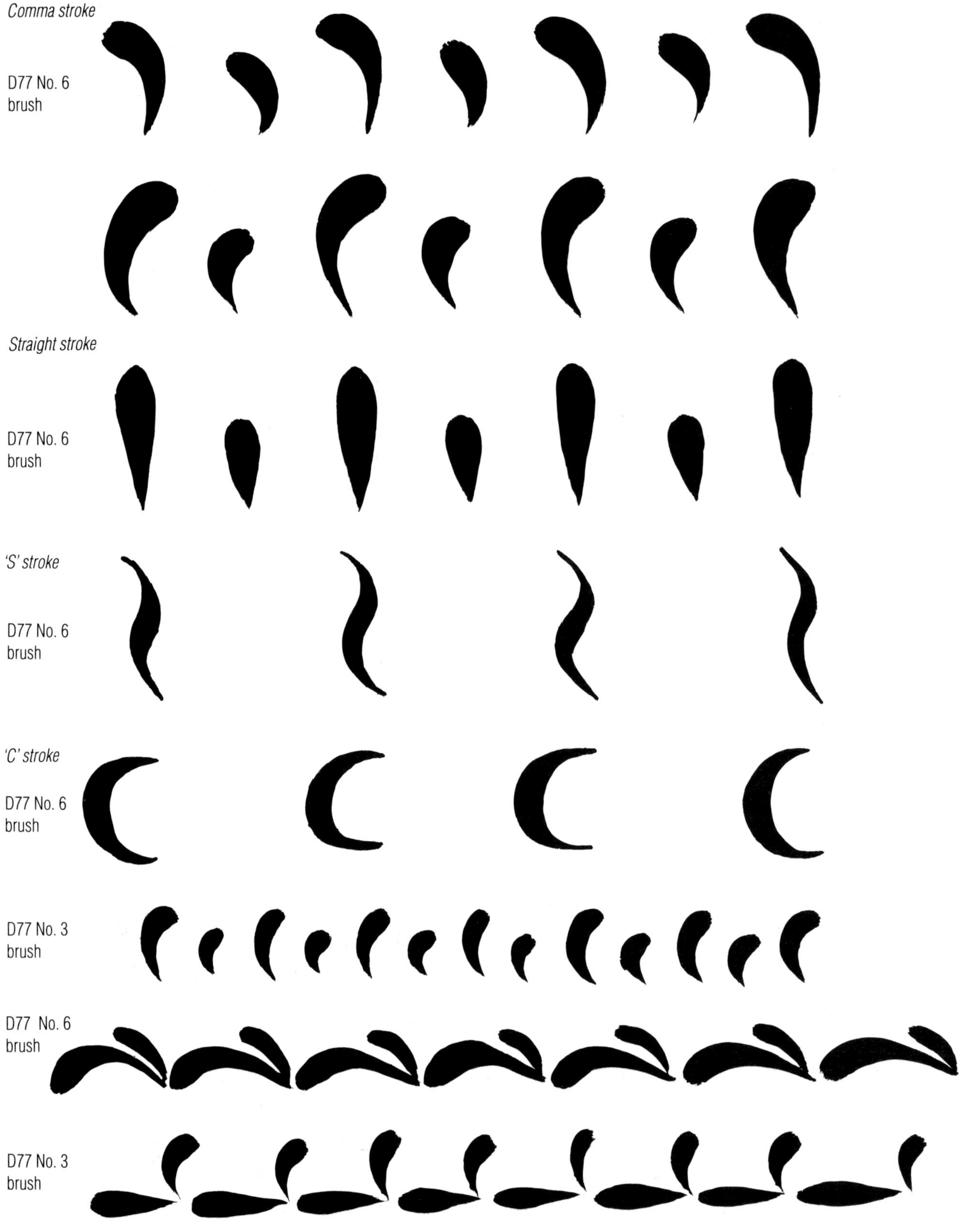

34

Comma stroke

D77 No. 6
brush

Straight stroke

D77 No. 6
brush

'S' stroke

D77 No. 6
brush

'C' stroke

D77 No. 6
brush

D77 No. 3
brush

D77 No. 6
brush

D77 No. 3
brush

FIG. 11
Round brush strokes worksheet

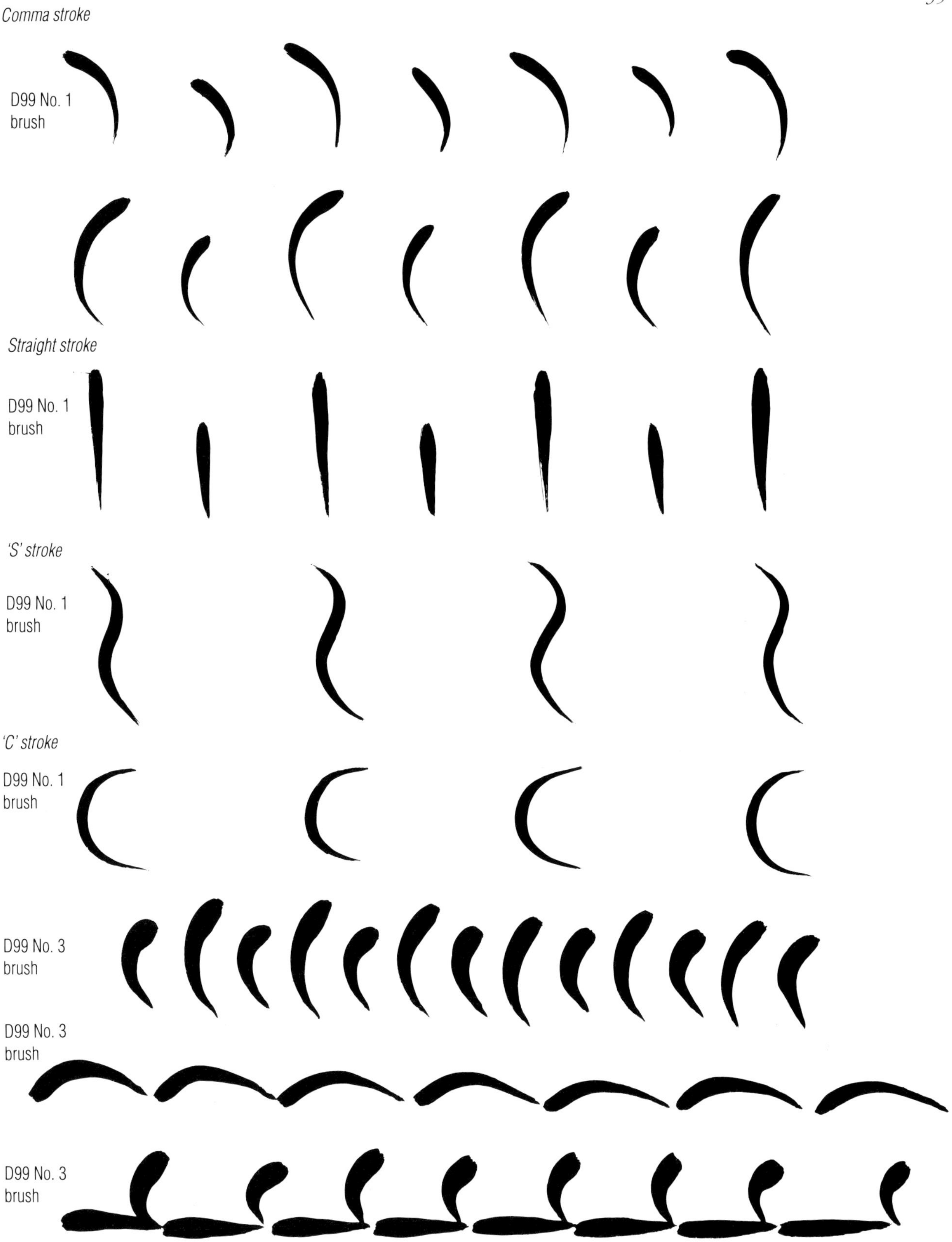

Comma stroke

D99 No. 1
brush

Straight stroke

D99 No. 1
brush

'S' stroke

D99 No. 1
brush

'C' stroke

D99 No. 1
brush

D99 No. 3
brush

D99 No. 3
brush

D99 No. 3
brush

FIG. 12
Rigger and liner brush strokes worksheet

Rigger and liner brush strokes worksheet

Comma stroke

1 Place the brush just slightly below the top of the comma stroke on the worksheet and add pressure to spread the brush hairs.

2 Gradually pull the brush towards you, releasing the pressure by lifting the brush, until it is finally on its tip at the end of the stroke. Stop and lift the brush. Notice how the shape of your stroke depends entirely on pressure and release. Do not twist the brush.

Straight stroke

1 Place the brush slightly below the top of the brush stroke on the worksheet and add pressure to the brush to spread the hairs.

2 Gradually release pressure while pulling the brush towards you. At the same time slightly twist the brush by pushing your thumb forwards against it. Finally finish on the tip of the brush.

Note: If you have difficulty with lifting, pulling and twisting in step 2, leave out the twisting and add the twist when you have perfected the lifting and pulling.

'S' stroke

1 Keep the paint smooth all round the tip of the brush and start to paint a thin line, gradually increasing pressure in the first curve of the stroke and keeping that pressure until the brush comes out of the second curve.

2 Gradually release pressure, finishing on the tip of the brush.

'C' stroke

Keep the paint smooth all round the tip of the brush and paint a thin line. Slowly add pressure with the most pressure in the centre of the 'C', then slowly lift the brush, finishing on the tip.

Flat brush strokes worksheet

Comma stroke

1 Place the chisel edge of the brush just slightly below the top of the comma stroke on the worksheet and add pressure to spread the brush hairs.

2 Gradually pull the brush towards you without twisting your wrist, and slowly release pressure by lifting your brush until it is finally on its chisel edge at the end of the stroke.

Straight stroke

1 Place the flat side of the brush slightly below the top of the brush stroke on the worksheet and add pressure to the brush to spread the hairs.

2 Gradually release pressure while pulling the brush towards you. At the same time slightly twist the brush by pushing your thumb forwards against it. Finally finish on the chisel edge of the brush.

'S' stroke

1 Keep the paint smooth on both sides of the flat brush.

2 Place the chisel edge of the brush at the beginning of the 'S' stroke. Slowly add pressure as you follow the shape of the 'S' stroke, with the most pressure in the two curves.

3 Slowly release pressure, returning to the chisel edge of the brush.

'C' stroke

1 Keep the paint smooth on either side of the flat brush.

2 Place the chisel edge of the brush at the beginning of the 'C' stroke. Slowly add pressure as you follow the shape of the 'C', exerting most pressure in the centre of the 'C'.

3 Slowly release pressure, returning to the chisel edge of the brush.

Problem solving

If after continued practice you are still not happy with your brush strokes, check that you have:

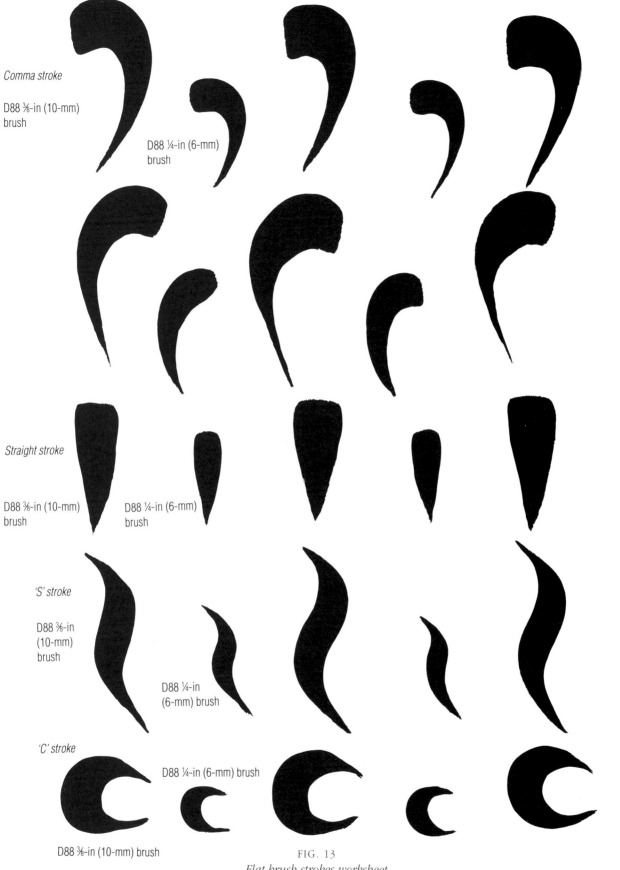

Comma stroke

D88 ⅜-in (10-mm) brush

D88 ¼-in (6-mm) brush

Straight stroke

D88 ⅜-in (10-mm) brush

D88 ¼-in (6-mm) brush

'S' stroke

D88 ⅜-in (10-mm) brush

D88 ¼-in (6-mm) brush

'C' stroke

D88 ¼-in (6-mm) brush

D88 ⅜-in (10-mm) brush

FIG. 13
Flat brush strokes worksheet

- the correct paint consistency;
- loaded the correct brush and followed the correct loading procedure;
- used the correct amount of pressure and release;
- stopped at the end of the brush stroke and then lifted your brush carefully.

New brushes need breaking in just like a pair of shoes, so the more you practise, the better your brush will work for you.

Master the basic brush strokes before attempting the more difficult strokes in Chapter 8.

TRACING AND TRANSFERRING A DESIGN PATTERN

For transferring patterns you will require: a fine black drawing pen, tracing paper, transfer paper, a stylus or empty ballpoint pen and masking tape.

Two kinds of paper are involved in transferring a pattern:

- tracing paper, the transparent paper used when making a copy of the pattern;
- transfer paper, which leaves the traced pattern marks on your piece of metal or wood. This paper consists of a coated surface of fine particles, usually consisting of either coloured chalk or grey carbon.

Wax-free transfer paper is produced in various colours, but you need to be aware that the colour can bleed from some coloured transfer papers. Always choose a contrasting colour that will give you good definition. Grey graphite and white are the most useful. Do not use blue, office-style, carbon-copy paper.

Transfer paper is available both by the roll and in sheets. If using sheets, you will need to move the paper around when tracing large patterns. For smaller patterns, cut the transfer paper into convenient sizes. Store the transfer paper in a folder to keep it flat and dry. One sheet of paper in continual use can last a year!

It is possible to make your own transfer paper if you cannot find it in an art or craft store. This can be done by following the directions below for tracing the pattern, but instead of placing transfer paper underneath your tracing, rub the back of the tracing with chalk or a pencil. Dust off any loose particles before commencing to trace on to the object.

Never transfer a design directly from this book on to an object as you will spoil the pattern in the book by marking it. Always first trace the design from the page on to tracing paper. If you are a beginner, you will probably have the tendency to follow every line. The lines you are tracing are merely a guide and, with experience, you will become accustomed to leaving out the detail, finding it easier to paint freehand.

It is advisable to omit stamens from flowers, for example, and all dots, overstrokes, scrolls and cross-hatching as these can be painted freehand. Study the lines you are tracing, so they are not just random lines, but forms that mean something. It is a good idea to develop a systematic approach so that important lines on the design are not omitted.

Procedure for tracing and transferring a design pattern

1(a) **Flat surfaces** such as trays, plates, shelves and so on. Make sure that the tracing paper is large enough to cover the surface of the object. Place the tracing paper under the object that will receive the design and, with a sharp pencil, trace around the object to get the size of the area for the transfer. Remove the tracing paper. As it is important to have the design pattern central, fold the tracing paper in half, both ways, to find the centre. Place the tracing paper over the pattern to be traced, carefully lining up the centre of the pattern and the centre of the tracing paper. Trace the pattern on to the tracing paper with a fine black drawing pen.

(b) **Round surfaces** such as waste-paper bins, planters, milk churns and so on. Make sure that the tracing paper is larger than the pattern to be traced. Trace the pattern on to the tracing paper with a fine black drawing pen.

2 Secure the traced pattern to the object using masking tape. Leave one side open so that the transfer paper can be slipped underneath the tracing.

3 Place the transfer paper under the tracing paper with the coloured side touching the object. Secure with masking tape.

4 With a stylus or an empty ballpoint pen, carefully go over the lines. Check that you have traced all the pattern before removing the papers and masking tape.

ADAPTING
DESIGN PATTERNS

Invariably patterns will be the wrong size to fit the object you wish to paint. Pattern size can be changed using photocopying enlargement or reduction, in which case change the brush sizes accordingly. Alternatively you can make your pattern larger simply by adding to it as I have done on the drawers in Project 13. Each drawer was slightly different in size from the next. As they increased in size, from the top to the bottom, I gradually increased the pattern by adding a few extra leaves to make it wider. By the time the bottom drawer had been reached, the gap on either side of the pattern was too great for any more leaves, so I painted four 'S' strokes for the ribbons as a filler.

You will notice that there is also a design on top of the chest. For this I traced some of the flowers taken from parts of the pattern used on the drawers and again added ribbons.

Groups of flowers taken from a pattern can be traced separately on to small objects. Usually a group of three flowers works well, as can be seen by the flowers in 'Crescent brush strokes' (page 47).

Adapt designs and create your own by adding or removing flowers or leaves to make patterns larger or smaller. If you wish to place different flowers in an existing pattern,

Design on top of chest of drawers

simply trace all the leaves and draw circles for the new flower positions. Place the new flowers under the traced circle and move them around until you are happy with their position. Trace the new flowers on to your new pattern.

Note: When replacing flowers, keep to the same art form. For instance, the Bavarian tulips in Project 11 can be exchanged for Bavarian chrysanthemums but *not* for English roses.

CHAPTER 7

Brush techniques

··

As you progress through the projects you will be learning new techniques, so will need to refer to this section and practise the relevant techniques before you start painting each design. See the illustration on page 41.

DOTS

Painting a perfect dot is a technique. Many paintings with flawless brush strokes can be spoilt by untidy dots, yet enhanced by good ones.

The secret of painting a flawless dot is in the consistency of the paint and in *not* using the brush hairs. There are a number of suitable implements and these are a few I have found successful:

- ❧ **Cocktail sticks** are useful for tiny dots.
- ❧ **Bamboo skewers** Both ends can be used for tiny and medium dots.
- ❧ **Erasers** on the end of pencils and **brush handles** of various sizes are useful for larger dots.

It is worthwhile experimenting with items which you think suitable for painting dots.

For the decorative folk painter dots are a blessing as they can be used to fill in any empty spaces, or to enhance flowers and make delicate borders.

Procedure for painting dots

1 Paint taken straight from the tube or jar is usually of too thick a consistency for dots and will leave a 'knob' on your painting. Make sure that the paint is the consistency of cream soup by adding just a drop or two of water and mixing with a brush handle or equivalent implement. Test the consistency of the paint by placing the tip of the brush *handle* into the paint and then removing it. If a peak mark remains in the paint in the position where brush handle was removed, the paint is too thick; in these circumstances slowly add a tiny drop of water to the paint. Should the paint start to 'bleed' on

the palette, you have been too generous with the water, so start again!

2 Place the stick or handle, which is to make the dot, into the paint and pick up the paint. Dab the end of the stick or handle, complete with paint, on to the painting.

3 For dots of even size, reload the brush for each dot.

4 For dots in descending order of size, load the stick or handle and paint dots without reloading. Normally up to five descending dots can be painted with one loading.

STIPPLING

For a stippling effect you will need a round bristle or stencil brush. It is best to stipple around a pattern and not in the areas where flowers or leaves are to be painted. Stippling does not leave a smooth surface and can be seen and felt through any overpainting. I have used stippling around the sweet peas in Project 14. For this design I dipped the stippling brush into two colours at once.

Procedure for stippling

1 Holding the brush upright, load it by dipping it into the paint.

2 Dab the brush on a piece of kitchen paper to remove any excess paint.

3 Hold the brush at 90 degrees and dab the surface area lightly with the bristles. Carry on dabbing until the brush needs reloading.

4 Repeat steps 1–3, changing colours when necessary.

TIPPING

Any shape or size of brush can be used for tipping. After you have loaded the brush with the main colour, dip the

BRUSH TECHNIQUES

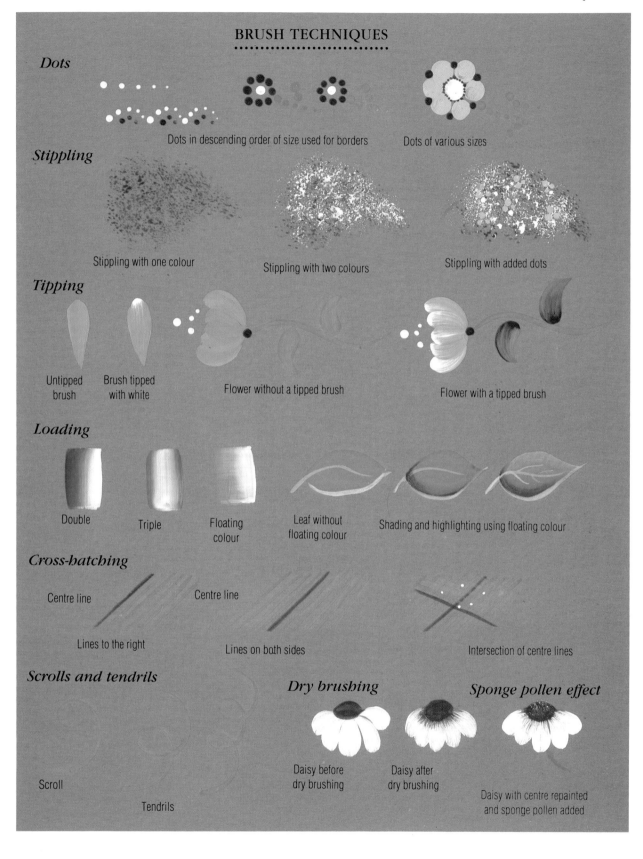

Dots

Dots in descending order of size used for borders

Dots of various sizes

Stippling

Stippling with one colour

Stippling with two colours

Stippling with added dots

Tipping

Untipped brush

Brush tipped with white

Flower without a tipped brush

Flower with a tipped brush

Loading

Double

Triple

Floating colour

Leaf without floating colour

Shading and highlighting using floating colour

Cross-hatching

Centre line

Centre line

Lines to the right

Lines on both sides

Intersection of centre lines

Scrolls and tendrils

Dry brushing

Sponge pollen effect

Scroll

Tendrils

Daisy before dry brushing

Daisy after dry brushing

Daisy with centre repainted and sponge pollen added

tip or chisel edge of the brush into another colour. The colour on the tip of the brush is the first to appear when painting, followed by the main colour: for instance, a brush loaded with blue paint and then dipped into white will give a stroke showing white fading into blue. This brush technique is simple, yet very effective and colourful. It is ideal for daisy and chrysanthemum petals and leaves, creating a subtle colour change. Experiment with colours as this is fun.

Procedure for tipping

1 Load the brush with the main colour.

2 Dip the tip of a round brush, or chisel edge if using a flat brush, into a contrasting colour of paint. Be sure to have just a small amount of paint on the brush hairs and not a 'blob'.

3 Paint the brush stroke as indicated by the pattern.

4 There is no need to wash the brush between strokes, but just reload it in the same way for each new stroke.

Note: For certain flowers in the Bavarian style of painting, paint well loaded on the tip of the brush is desirable to achieve the required effect.

DOUBLE LOADING

Double loading is an excellent way of painting colourful strokes. The brush is loaded with two colours: for example, a brush loaded with blue and white will, when blended on the palette, produce a gradual change in colour from blue through pale blue to white. Only flat brushes are suitable for double loading and it is advisable to have plenty of room on your palette for blending. In the projects I have used double loading for primroses and sweet peas.

Procedure for double loading

1 Wash a flat brush, preferably ¼ in (6 mm) or ⅜ in (10 mm) in size, with clean water and wipe lightly against a piece of kitchen paper.

2 Load one paint colour on one half of the brush by pushing the *knife edge* forwards into the paint half-way up the brush hairs.

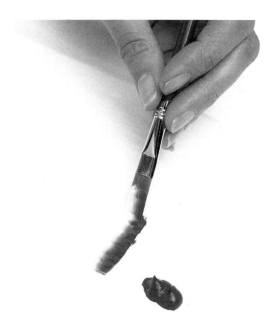

Double loading a brush

3 Load a second paint colour on the opposite knife edge of the brush in the same way.

4 Blend the two colours together on a clean section of the wet palette by stroking the brush five times on its flat side, from left to right. Repeat the procedure from right to left using the other side of the brush.

There are two alternative ways of stroking the brush through the palette which give different effects:

(a) You should make sure that the blending strokes are all done on the exact same area of the palette: that is, if you are using blue and white, the blue side of the brush is blending on the blue line created on the palette, and the white paint on the white line. You should be hitting the palette in a section exactly the width of the brush and about 2 in (5 cm) long and going over that exact same area each time. When you reverse, keep to the same colour side by wiping in the other direction of stroke.

(b) For a softer blend of colour you can walk the brush away from the colour line when pulling the brush through on the palette. Only do this by moving the brush slightly towards you, therefore overlapping by about ⅛ in (3 mm), and pull it on a course parallel to the first stroke. When reversing, use the same brush position and wipe in the opposite direction of the stroke.

Note: For the very first double loading of the brush only, you will need to repeat steps 2, 3 and 4 once more. This will ensure that the brush is fully loaded.

5 Paint the brush stroke as required by the pattern.

6 Reload the brush using the same method for every brush stroke in the pattern, without washing the brush in between strokes. It is necessary to wash the brush only when changing colours or if the following occurs:

(a) the brush hairs become dry around the ferrule and the movement of the brush becomes impaired; or

(b) the colours are inadvertently picked up on the wrong sides.

Note: If you do not use the same spot on the palette for the blending, you will (a) run out of paint, as not only is paint put on to the palette, but it is also retrieved; and, (b) pick up another colour by mistake!

TRIPLE LOADING

Triple loading requires a ¼-in (6-mm) or ⅜-in (10-mm) flat brush. The brush is loaded with three different colours, or two colours in three areas. The triple colour is achieved by loading the brush with the main colour, and then adding two different colours, one on either side. Triple loading is a little more difficult to achieve but, once accomplished, this produces very effective brush strokes. I have used the technique for the uppermost petal in the honeysuckle in Project 6. You will notice that this petal consists of a main colour, burgundy, which is loaded on to the brush, and then the two outside edges of the brush are loaded with white and blended again. This produces a brush stroke with a gradual change of colour from white to pink to burgundy, then back to pink and white again.

Procedure for triple loading

1 Wash a flat brush in clean water and wipe gently against a piece of kitchen paper.

2 Load all the brush hairs with the chosen main colour.

3 Load the outside edges only with the chosen colours by pushing each knife edge into the paint. Make sure that the centre of the brush hairs still show the main colour and it has not been obliterated by the two colours added on the outside edges.

4 Blend the two outside colours into the main colour. Do this on a clean area of the wet palette by wiping the brush gently twice on one flat side, pulling it from left to right, and then on the other side from right to left. Keep the brush on the same colour stripe in the palette: for example, if using burgundy, keep the burgundy brush hairs on the burgundy blending line.

Blending in triple loading is the same as in double loading apart from the following two important aspects:

(a) Use only a minimal number of strokes to blend (two each side is suggested), otherwise the effects of the graduation of colour will be lost when the brush stroke is painted.

(b) The softer blending technique described in 4(b) in 'Double loading' (page 42) is *not* suitable. This would result in too much loss of graduated colour effect when the stroke is painted.

FLOATING COLOUR

Floating colour is sometimes referred to as side loading. I prefer the term 'floating colour' as the brush work is nearly always painted on top of an already coloured area – for example, on a leaf. The transparency of the floating colour allows the original paint colour underneath to show through in a graded relief. I have used the technique for many of the projects. Project 15, depicting poppies, uses floating colour for highlighting and shading, as this gives added depth to the flower petals.

For shading, a darker colour than the underlying colour is added to a clean, wet brush and loaded with paint on one side only. The paint is then blended on the wet palette. For example, a brush loaded with dark green paint on one side can be used to shade a light green leaf. The effect is to shade the leaf from dark green, fading through the transparency of the water, to the original light green.

For highlighting, a paint of lighter colour than the underlying colour is used and applied in exactly the same manner as for shading.

Shading and highlighting can be applied on opposite sides of a leaf, for example, to give a very realistic effect.

I have used the floating colour technique slightly differently on the satin ribbon in Project 19. For this effect the brush is loaded with white floating colour and one short brush stroke is painted. Then the brush is flipped over and immediately another brush stroke is made so that the paint edge of the brush touches the paint edge of the preceding stroke. The edges that so meet in the ribbon example are the white edges and this has created a shiny strip as if the ribbon were gleaming like satin at that point.

Floating colour does not always have to be an overlay technique. It can be used for the original painting of petals and leaves when a soft edge effect is required.

The D88 ⅜-in (10-mm) brush is the most flexible to use for floating colour and you will find that it is not necessary to reload the brush for each stroke.

Procedure for floating colour

1 Wash the brush with clean water and wipe gently across a piece of kitchen paper so as not to remove too much water from the brush hairs, but ensuring that the ferrule area is dry.

2 Load the flat brush by pushing one knife edge only into the paint.(The other side of the brush is in effect already loaded with water.)

3 Blend the water and paint together on the wet palette by wiping the flat side of the brush three times from left to right. Reverse the brush and blend three times as in the double loading technique, keeping the water on the water side and the paint on the paint side on the wet palette. Blending for floating colour is done in exactly the same way as for double loading (see section 4(a) and (b), page 42), except that not so many strokes are used.

4 Check for excess paint on the knife edge of the brush and remove. Add a touch more water if the brush becomes dry.

5 Paint the brush strokes indicated by the pattern.

Note: At the end of the brush stroke, especially when the brush is a little wet, it is quite normal to find a water or brush mark left that you don't want. Dab this with your finger and the mark will disappear into a soft edge.

CROSS-HATCHING
••••••••••••••••••••

Cross-hatching is a group of parallel lines, intersected by another group of parallel lines so that diamond shapes are formed. Cross-hatching is used in the Pennsylvania Dutch design in Project 20.

Procedure for cross-hatching

1 Do not trace lines for cross-hatching.

2 Paint the lines using a liner brush, No. 1 or 0 depending on the size of the object you are painting.

3 Keep a steady pressure on the brush as the strokes need to be evenly painted.

4 The paint should run fluidly, so add a few drops of water or flow medium to the paint to make it the same consistency as used for painting dots (that of cream soup).

5 The brush should be kept loaded so that the lines do not start fading away but retain the same depth of colour.

6 As cross-hatching does not form squares but diamond shapes, it is useful to note the following:
(a) Paint the first line slightly off centre in the area to be cross-hatched. On the worksheet this line is shown darker to identify it.
(b) Continue to paint parallel lines on one side of the first line until that side of the shape has been filled in.
(c) Continue painting on the other side of the first line in the same manner.

7 To ensure that you make diamond shapes, place a ruler at right angles to the first line, then swing the ruler round slightly so that you can be sure that the second set of lines is not at a right angle to the first set.

8 Repeat the diagonals in the opposite direction as in steps 6(b) and (c).

Note: After you have accomplished cross-hatching with a ruler, practise freehand.

SPONGE BLENDING
••••••••••••••••••••

Sponge blending is using a sponge to blend paints which have already been applied to a design. This gives a more uniform and textured effect than when using a brush. The technique has been used for the strawberries in Project 9 and all the fruit on the mixed fruit tray in Project 10. Practise first before attempting to paint either design.

You will need a pair of tweezers and tiny pieces of synthetic sponge (do not use foam as the holes are too close together). It is not necessary to wash the brush when working on a specific fruit; just wipe it on kitchen paper and reload. While blending, place your brush on a piece of damp kitchen paper or flat sponge, thus keeping the paint on the brush moist.

It is important to paint one fruit at a time, preparing tiny pieces of sponge ready to be placed in the tweezers. You will need retarder for all the fruit in Project 10 apart from the grapes as they are very small and I find that there is sufficient time for blending before the paint dries.

Procedure for sponge blending

1 When using this technique for fruit, as in Projects 9 and 10, undercoat all the fruit as described in the project instructions and allow to dry. (Some fruit will require two undercoats and this should be allowed to dry before you proceed to step 2).

2 Brush or smear a thin layer of retarder over the surface of the fruit to be blended.

3 Lightly touch this area with a piece of kitchen paper to remove any excess retarder.

4 Paint generously using the brush and colours indicated by the pattern.

5 You will be blending the dark colours first and the highlight last. Place a small piece of sponge in the tweezers and hold the tweezers. With the sponge, *lightly* dab the fruit all round the circumference, gradually working towards the centre. Continue in this way until all painted lines have been blended. Replace the sponge regularly with a new piece as it picks up paint from the surface.

Problem solving

- **Paint becomes transparent** The remedy here is to use less retarder or blot the surface more with the kitchen paper.
- **Colours blended become one colour** Should this happen, you may need to change the sponge more frequently. It may also be possible that you are over-sponging: stop sponging while you can still see the original colours.
- **Brush marks show where colours should appear blended** It is possible that insufficient retarder was left on the surface and this has caused the paint to dry quickly before you were able to sponge blend. Use a little more retarder, making sure that you cover the outside edges of the fruit.

- **Edges of fruit look untidy** Probably due to the fact that the sponge pieces are too big. Rectify this by using smaller pieces of sponge. For the immediate problem, use the liner brush with the same colour paint as the fruit and paint flowing lines around the edges.

SPONGE POLLEN EFFECT FOR FLOWER CENTRES

Lightly touching a flower centre with a piece of sponge dipped into paint can transform not only the flower, but also the painting. I used this technique for the majority of daisies in the projects.

You will need tweezers and tiny pieces of either foam or synthetic sponge.

Procedure for sponge pollen effect for flower centres

1 Paint the flower centre according to the project instructions and allow to dry.

2 Place a piece of sponge in the tweezers.

3 Holding the sponge in the tweezers, lightly touch it in the appropriate colour for pollen (this can be cream, yellow or gold). Lightly dab the sponge on to kitchen paper to remove excess paint, as you need a very light imprint left on the flower centre.

4 Pat the flower centre once or twice with the sponge until the desired effect has been achieved.

5 Repeat steps 2 and 3, if necessary.

SCROLLS AND TENDRILS

Scrolls can be painted with a flat, liner or round brush. For the rosemaling design in Project 16 a flat brush was used. In the colour illustration on page 41, scrolls are demonstrated with a liner brush. Scrolls can be continued with a looping effect to become tendrils. These brush strokes can be used in conjunction with dots to fill in empty gaps in a design. A few liner brush scrolls can help balance a design if you have unfortunately placed your pattern off centre.

Procedure for painting scrolls

1 Make sure that the paint is fluid: that is, of the consistency of cream soup. If you run out of paint before the end of the brush stroke, you will need to add more water or flow medium next time.

2 Load a D99 No. 1 or a No. 0 liner brush.

3 Hold the brush at 90 degrees to the paper and slowly pull it, adding pressure as you move into the swirl and releasing pressure as you finish the stroke.

4 Repeat the process if you wish to have two swirls. Every swirl of the brush should produce smooth curves and no sharp corners. The quicker you make the brush stroke, the better.

SIMPLE DRY BRUSHING

A simple type of dry brushing has been used for the nasturtiums in Project 8 and the Hindeloopen bird in Project 12. Here you are simply 'scratching' paint on to the flower with a dry brush. The brush is loaded with paint and brushed a few times across the palette to remove excess paint so that it is virtually dry. Then, with the brush hairs splayed, dry brushing is applied as indicated by the project instructions, using the tips of the hairs only.

DRY BRUSHING FOR FLOWER CENTRES

The effect of dry brushing in the centre of flowers can make even a dull daisy come alive! With this technique you are pulling paint rather than 'scratching' it. The technique has been used on the spinner's chair in Project 5.

You will need one or two completely dry brushes. A D77 No. 3 or other low-numbered brush works well.

Procedure for dry brushing flower centres

1 Add retarder to the paint which is to be dry brushed.

2 Paint the flower centre as indicated by the project instructions.

3 Use a dry brush. Hold the brush at the bottom of the ferrule area with your thumb and first finger. Press these two fingers together so that the pressure on the hairs forces the hairs to spread like a fan.

4 Using the *tips* of the brush hairs only, drag the paint from the flower centre towards you. It is important to remember to pull the paint towards you, so you must turn the design round as you work to enable this. Each pull of the brush should drag the paint on to a petal in the direction of the petal brush stroke. Wipe the dry brush on kitchen paper between strokes to prevent the accumulation of paint.

5 Continue dry brushing until the whole area to be covered is complete.

6 When the paint is dry, repaint the flower centre without using retarder.

Problem solving

- Paint cannot be dragged as it has dried To remedy this problem add more retarder to the paint.
- Paint has not spread evenly after dry brushing Try fanning the brush hairs more, using a fresh brush or less pressure.

CHAPTER 8

More complex brush strokes

CRESCENT BRUSH STROKES

Numerous forms of crescent stroke can be devised from the basic crescent stroke by changing the direction and pressure of the brush before finishing the stroke. There are four variations on the basic crescent: the dipped crescent, the ruffled crescent, the pointed crescent and the jagged crescent. Another five brush strokes can be devised from this list simply by making each brush stroke from the list into a closed crescent. Add to this five more longer, elongated strokes, and we now have fifteen different brush strokes!

Worksheets are provided for all these various crescent brush strokes; as suggested on page 33, you may prefer to photocopy the worksheets instead of working direct from the book. The first row on each worksheet shows the specified crescent brush stroke. The second row depicts the same brush stroke but closed. The third row shows the same brush stroke as the second row but longer and therefore called 'elongated'.

At the bottom of each worksheet are examples of how these brush strokes can be used, mainly in conjunction with double loading. I have painted dots and comma strokes to enhance the designs and I am sure that you will enjoy devising different combinations to make your own designs.

All crescent strokes require a flat brush either ¼-in (6-mm) or ⅜-in (10 mm) in size. I have used the D88 ⅜ in (10 mm) brush for all the crescents apart from the jagged crescent; for this I have used the Prolene 106 ⅜ in (10 mm) brush. For crescent strokes it is especially important that the brush is as soft as it was when new, because these strokes use the brush to the limit of its flexibility. Crescent strokes are used mainly for flower petals and leaves. All strokes start and finish on the chisel edge of the brush.

I have used a clock-face method in describing how to achieve these strokes and have suggested start positions of five to or ten to the hour to indicate the sort of sweep arc needed. However, as always in art, common sense will indicate that these strokes can be swept wider to achieve different effects, so do not be bound by these values.

The brush can be loaded with one, two or three colours, but two colours provide the best effect and this is what I have used for the worksheets and projects.

BASIC CRESCENT

The basic crescent brush stroke uses more pressure than the 'C' stroke and it is painted as an arch shape with the open end of the crescent facing the bottom of the page. See the colour illustration overleaf.

Procedure for painting the basic crescent

1 Double load a D88 ⅜-in (10-mm) brush with white and red paint. Blend the paint well as in normal double loading.

2 Hold the flat brush on the chisel edge, at a steep angle about 80 degrees to the work surface. Look at the photograph below to help gauge the angle and position of the brush when starting and finishing the stroke. Set

Starting position and angle of the brush for the basic crescent stroke

BASIC CRESCENT BRUSH STROKES WORKSHEET

Basic crescent

Closed crescent

Elongated closed crescent

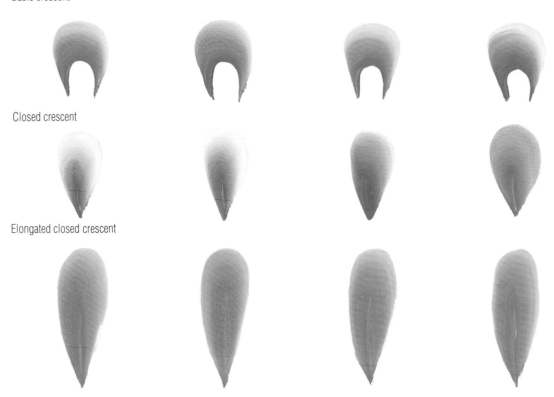

For both flowers the brush was loaded with Cadmium Red Deep and Titanium White and well blended. The flower on the left had the red paint leading and the flower on the right had the pink paint leading. For the leaves the brush was loaded with Titanium White and Opaque Oxide of Chromium with white leading.

Elongated closed crescent

Closed crescent

Basic crescent

Closed crescent

Elongated closed crescent

the chisel edge on the surface so that a line drawn through it will run up to the 'five to' position (imagine a clock face and use the times as position markers). The corner of the brush which starts nearest to you when you begin the stroke is the corner which *remains nearest throughout the stroke.*

3 Sweep the brush (with white paint leading) forwards to the 'five to' position. Start the stroke with minimum pressure on the brush and build increasing pressure (as shown in the photograph below) until the 'twelve o'clock' position when you need to relax the pressure as you sweep back round through the 'five past' position and on to the clock centre, such that you match the pressure used on the upward stroke. Note that as the downward stroke is executed the red paint is now on the

Building pressure during the basic crescent stroke

leading edge of the brush.

4 The final effect should be a crescent stroke with white all the way around the outside and red on the inside. The outward and backward strokes should be mirror images of each other in colour and pressure.

Closed and elongated basic crescents

Use the same movement as for the basic crescent, but start and finish at the same point in the absolute clock centre position.

DIPPED CRESCENT

The dipped crescent brush stroke is pretty much the same as the basic crescent, but the brush is pulled towards you and then swept back out again in the centre of the stroke to create a dip effect at the outer rim of the crescent. See the colour illustration overleaf. This brush stroke is ideal for petals of flowers of the *Primula* family, such as the primrose in Project 7.

Procedure for painting the dipped crescent

1 Double load a D88 ⅜-in (10-mm) brush with white and yellow paint. Blend the paint well as in normal double loading.

2 Hold the flat brush on the chisel edge, at a steep angle about 80 degrees to the work surface. Look at the photograph on page 47 to help gauge the angle and position of the brush when starting and finishing the stroke. Set the chisel edge on the surface so that a line drawn through it will run up to the 'five to' position (imagine a clock face and use the times as position markers). The corner of the brush which starts nearest to you when you begin the stroke is the corner which *remains nearest throughout the stroke.*

3 Sweep the brush (with white paint leading) forwards to the 'five to' position. Start the stroke with minimum pressure on the brush and build pressure gradually until nearly at the 'twelve o'clock' position when you pull the brush towards you, slightly releasing pressure and making a dip in the stroke. As you reach the bottom of the dip, bring the brush up into a vertical position: the chisel edge should just be resting on the surface. Sweep the brush back up to the clock rim, resuming the pressure and brush angle as you do so. You need to relax the pressure again as you sweep back round through the 'five past' position and on towards the clock centre, such that you match the pressure used on the upward stroke. Note that as the downward stroke is executed, the yellow paint is now on the leading edge of the brush.

4 The final effect should be a dipped crescent stroke with white all the way around the outside and yellow on the inside. The outward and backward strokes should be mirror images of each other in colour and pressure.

DIPPED CRESCENT BRUSH STROKES WORKSHEET

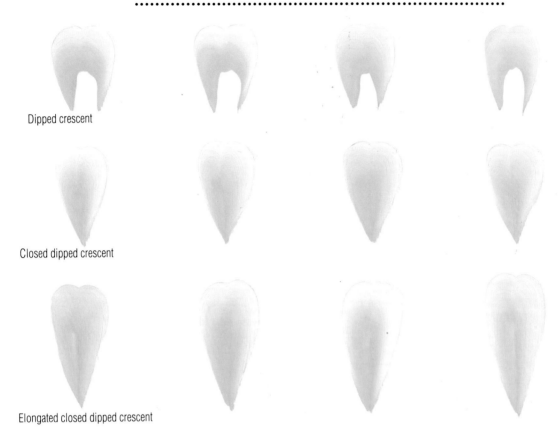

Dipped crescent

Closed dipped crescent

Elongated closed dipped crescent

For the flowers on the left the brush was loaded with Cadmium Yellow and Cadmium Yellow Deep. Cadmium Yellow was leading. For the flowers on the right the brush was loaded with Cadmium Yellow Deep and Titanium White, with Cadmium Yellow Deep leading. The leaves were painted with Opaque Oxide of Chromium and Titanium White, with a touch of Cadmium Yellow Deep added to the leaves on the left.

Closed dipped crescent

Closed dipped crescent

Closed dipped crescent

Elongated closed dipped crescent

RUFFLED CRESCENT BRUSH STROKES WORKSHEET

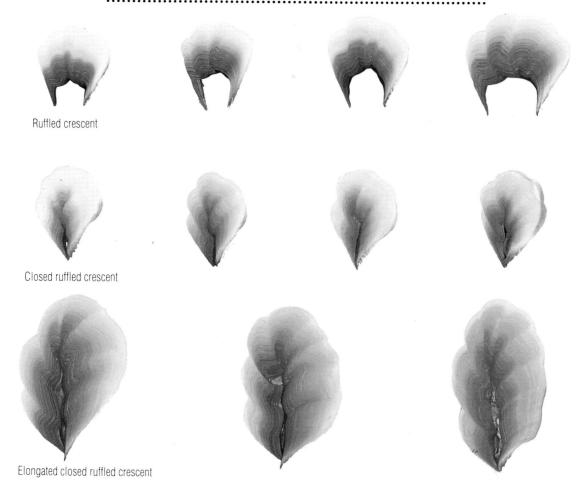

Ruffled crescent

Closed ruffled crescent

Elongated closed ruffled crescent

For both flowers the brush was loaded with Permanent Violet and Titanium White and well blended. For both flowers violet was the leading colour. For the leaves the brush was loaded with Titanium White and Opaque Oxide of Chromium. For the flower on the left white paint was leading and for the flower on the right Opaque Oxide of Chromium was leading.

Closed ruffled crescent

Closed ruffled crescent

Ruffled crescent

Closed ruffled crescent

Elongated closed ruffled crescent

Closed and elongated dipped crescents

Use the same movement as for the dipped crescent but start and finish at the same point in the absolute clock centre position.

RUFFLED CRESCENT

The ruffled crescent brush stroke is painted in a similar way to the basic crescent. Here the brush is manipulated in a bouncing action to give a ruffle effect around the edge of the sweep. See the colour illustration on page 51. The ruffled crescent is used for the sweet pea petals in Project 14.

Procedure for painting the ruffled crescent

1 Double load a D88 ⅜-in (10-mm) brush with white and purple paint. Blend the paint well as in normal double loading.

2 Hold the flat brush on the chisel edge, at a steep angle about 80 degrees to the work surface. Look at the photograph on page 47 to help gauge the angle and position of the brush when starting and finishing the brush stroke. Set the chisel edge on the surface so that a line drawn through it will run up to the 'five to' position (imagine a clock face and use the times as position markers). The corner of the brush which starts nearest to you when you begin the stroke is the corner which *remains nearest throughout the stroke.*

3 Sweep the brush (with white paint leading) forwards to the 'five to' position. Start the stroke with minimum pressure on the brush. Apply pressure and at the same time bounce the brush up and down to form ruffles, still following the basic crescent shape. Sweep on with the ruffle effect back round through the 'five past' position. Then release the pressure and sweep down, without ruffling, towards the clock centre, such that you match the pressure used on the upward stroke. Note that as the downward stroke is executed, the purple paint is now on the leading edge of the brush.

4 The final effect should be a ruffled crescent with white all the way around the outside and purple on the inside. The outward and backward strokes should be mirror images of each other in colour and pressure.

Closed and elongated ruffled crescents

Use the same movement as for the ruffled crescent but sweep upwards towards the 'ten to' position and back from the 'ten past' position in a wider shape. When ruffling, sweep the brush in tiny arcs to give larger ruffles and keep up the pressure when sweeping through the arc movement. Here, of course, the start and finish points are in the absolute clock centre position.

POINTED CRESCENT

The instructions for the pointed crescent look daunting, but it is well worthwhile trying to accomplish painting this brush stroke. The stroke is painted in the same way as for the basic crescent, but, when nearing the centre, the brush swings upwards. See the colour illustration opposite. Read each step carefully and keep practising. This stroke is used for the central fuchsia flower petals in Project 13.

Procedure for painting the pointed crescent

1 Double load a D88 ⅜-in (10 mm) brush with white and blue paint. Blend the paint well as in normal double loading.

2 Hold the flat brush on the chisel edge, at a steep angle about 80 degrees to the work surface. Look at the photograph on page 47 to help gauge the angle and position of the brush when starting and finishing the stroke. Set the chisel edge on the surface so that a line drawn through it will run up to the 'five to' position (imagine a clock face and use the times as position markers). The corner of the brush which starts nearest to you when you begin the stroke is the corner which *remains nearest throughout the stroke.*

3 Sweep the brush (with white paint leading) forwards toward the 'five to' position. Start the stroke with minimum pressure on the brush and build pressure gradually until nearing the 'twelve o'clock' position. Then swing the brush upwards to the 'twelve o'clock' point of the petal. As you reach the tip of the petal, release pressure and bring the brush up into a vertical position so that the chisel edge is just resting on the surface. Now pull the brush vertically downwards towards you, adding more pressure on the brush until the hairs are practically bent in half and resuming the brush angle of 80 degrees. Then you need to relax the pressure as you sweep back

POINTED CRESCENT BRUSH STROKES WORKSHEET

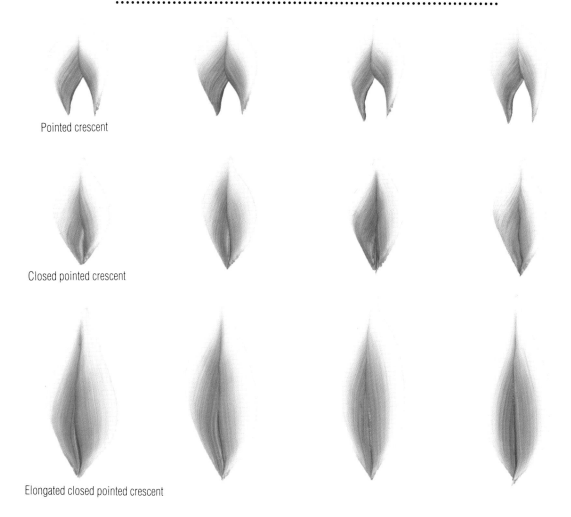

Pointed crescent

Closed pointed crescent

Elongated closed pointed crescent

The brush was loaded with Cobalt Blue and Titanium White for these periwinkles, with the blue paint leading. The green for the leaves was mixed using Cobalt Blue and Cadmium Yellow Deep.

Closed pointed crescent

round through the 'five past' position and on towards the clock centre, such that you match the pressure used on the upward stroke. Note that as the downward stroke is executed, the blue paint is now on the leading edge of the brush.

4 The final effect should be a pointed crescent stroke with white all the way around the outside and blue on the inside. The outward and backward strokes should be mirror images of each other in colour and pressure.

Closed and elongated pointed crescents

Use exactly the same movement as for the pointed crescent, but add more pressure when necessary. Note that the stroke begins and ends in the absolute clock centre position.

JAGGED CRESCENT

The jagged crescent brush stroke follows the same shape as the basic crescent but the brush needs to move quickly up and down while continuing the shape of the stroke. See the colour illustration opposite. This brush stroke has been used to form the carnation petals in Project 19.

Procedure for painting the jagged crescent

1 Double load a Prolene 106 ⅜-in (10-mm) brush with yellow and red. Blend the paint well as in normal double loading.

2 Hold the flat brush on the chisel edge, at a steep angle about 80 degrees to the work surface. Look at the photograph on page 47 to help gauge the angle and position of the brush when starting and finishing the brush stroke. Set the chisel edge on the surface so that a line drawn through it will run up to the 'five to' position (imagine a clock face and use the times as position markers). The corner of the brush which starts nearest to you when you begin the stroke is the corner which *remains nearest throughout the stroke.*

3 Sweep the brush (with red paint leading) forwards to the 'five to' position. Start the stroke with minimum pressure on the brush. Add very little pressure as you continue the stroke and, at the same time, move the brush quickly up and down, until you reach the centre of the curve. Gradually release any pressure but, at the same time, continue the momentum of the up-and-down movement following the crescent shape. Cease the movement and slide the brush towards the centre, finishing on the chisel edge with yellow leading.

4 The final effect should be a jagged crescent stroke with red all the way around the outside and yellow on the inside. The outward and backward strokes should be mirror images of each other in colour and pressure.

Closed and elongated jagged crescents

Use exactly the same movement as for the jagged crescent but make longer brush strokes. I have offset the elongated crescent on the worksheet: you may find this easier and also useful in some designs. Note that the stroke begins and ends in the absolute clock centre position.

Problem solving with crescent strokes

- **Wrong colour paint on the outside edge at the beginning or ending of the stroke** You will need to check the chisel edge angle of the brush or that the correct paint is at the top edge of the brush.
- **'Blobs' of paint on the outside edge at the end of the stroke** Check that you are releasing pressure slowly and returning on the chisel edge.
- **Difficulty in manoeuvring the brush** Rotation of the brush chisel edge in these strokes must be limited from the 'five to' position through 'twelve o'clock' and round to the 'five past' position. Often the impulse to swirl the brush head takes over. This temptation must be resisted as it results in the paint being in the wrong position on the flower petals or leaves.

JAGGED CRESCENT BRUSH STROKES WORKSHEET

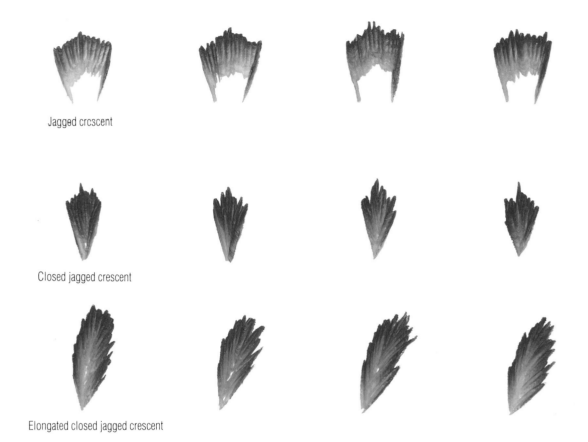

Jagged crescent

Closed jagged crescent

Elongated closed jagged crescent

For the flowers the brush was loaded with Vermilion (Hue) and Cadmium Yellow Deep. For the large flower on the right, Vermilion (Hue) was leading. For the small flowers on the left, Cadmium Yellow Deep was the leading colour. For the leaves, the brush was loaded with Titanium White and Opaque Oxide of Chromium with Opaque Oxide of Chromium leading.

Closed jagged crescent

Jagged crescent

Elongated closed jagged crescent

CHAPTER 9

Finishing touches

PROTECTING YOUR DECORATION

After all your hard work, your painting deserves to be protected. Ensure that the paint is completely dry, allowing at least a couple of days in a warm environment. If you have used retarder, the drying time will be longer even with the help of a hair dryer. I wait at least a week before varnishing any of my work.

Procedure for protecting your decoration

1 Check that all pattern lines and guide lines and any other marks have been removed. Use a damp cloth or cotton wool bud to remove chalk lines. Graphite lines are more stubborn, but I have found that pencil erasers or soap and water work well on these.

2 Apply varnish in two thin coats using a soft brush and allow plenty of drying time between coats.

3 After the second coat has dried, sand lightly with 600 wet-and-dry abrasive paper and wipe with a tack cloth to remove dust.

Note: If your item is purely non-functional, two coats of varnish are sufficient. For functional items apply up to four coats of varnish.

ANTIQUING AFTER VARNISHING

This kind of antiquing is not to be confused with antiquing before decoration (see page 24). Although they both serve to achieve an antiqued look, the methods are completely different. This form of antiquing is done at the final stages and involves making the actual painting look old as opposed to the background only. When antiquing,

you need to use an oil-based varnish both before and after the decoration. The item is then antiqued with oil paint and varnished again.

Antiquing is best suited to natural or stained wooden surfaces, but it can also be applied to dark painted backgrounds. The stained wooden stool in Project 9 has been antiqued.

Equipment

Tubes of Burnt Umber or Burnt Sienna oil paint.
Linseed oil (at room temperature)
Soft, lint-free cloth
Tack cloth
Cotton wool buds
Soft paint brush

Procedure for antiquing after varnishing

1 Follow the appropriate procedure for protecting your decoration (see left).

2 Pour a small amount of linseed oil on to a cloth and wipe the whole of the area to be antiqued, first wiping with the grain and then against it.

3 Squeeze a small amount of oil paint on to the oily spot on the cloth and apply the paint in the same way as the linseed oil.

4 Gently wipe the areas to be highlighted with either a clean cloth or cotton wool bud. Should the areas around the highlights form a hard edge, soften the edges by brushing lightly.

5 Allow at least one week to dry in a warm environment.

6 Apply one or two coats of varnish.

CHAPTER 10

Projects

COLOUR SENSE

Many of us have colour sense, yet there are also many people around who love painting, but who lack colour sense. The best way to develop this facility is to practise mixing colours.

To help you on your way with the projects in this chapter I have set out below a few hints which will ensure that all the colours you choose tone in well with your background colour.

- When painting on natural or stained wood, first recognize the colour of the wood. Mahogany or red stains will lend themselves to pinkish-toned designs, but the majority of woods and stains are best suited to warm palette colours – yellow, orange and brown.
- Should you choose a pastel shade for your painted background, you cannot go wrong if you remember the following:
  - All pastel shades contain white.
  - Mixing a touch of white paint into every colour chosen for your design will instantly change it into a pastel shade, thus toning with the pastel background.
- Similarly you can harmonize using the second colour which makes your pastel background. Decide which is the second colour by looking at the background again. If your pastel shade is pink, red is the second colour. If your pastel shade is pale blue, blue is the second colour. This second colour can be added to green paint to tone green foliage. Add the second colour sparingly.
- If you feel that your reds, greens and blues are too bright for the background colour, tone them down with just a touch of Payne's Grey or Burnt Umber.
- If your painting looks dull against the background, paint white dots and Burnt Umber brush strokes.
- Quite often there is more than one colour suitable for the background. As you will see, the colour illustrations have a different coloured background to the finished project.

SOURCES OF ARTICLES

Car boot sales, garage sales, flea markets and your own loft or cellar are the first places to look when hunting for old items to paint. Old metal and wooden trays are ideal when starting decorative painting as the surface is flat. The majority of old items used in the projects in this book were purchased at car boot sales.

While it feels good to stand back and admire an item of furniture you have renovated, it adds variety to paint a new piece. Craft and pine furniture shops sell new wooden items suitable for painting, or you can make your own: in the projects, woodwork patterns are included for the simpler wooden items – the spinner's chair, small paddle shape, clock, stool and cheese platter.

HOW TO PROCEED WITH THE PROJECTS

For each of the following projects there is: a pattern; a colour illustration; painting instructions; a colour photograph of the finished object; and patterns for making the base object (certain projects only). When following the painting instructions for the brush strokes, you will need to refer to the colour illustration and also any to black and white line illustrations.

It is important that you practise the techniques listed for each project before starting to paint. If you are a beginner, start at Project 1 and work through to Project 20. The brush strokes for each project are listed in order of difficulty, so it is recommended that you start with the easiest.

If you have done decorative painting before look at the table in Fig. 14 on page 59 to see which projects you can attempt after becoming familiar with each brush stroke. The table shows which techniques are needed for each project. Some projects may seem daunting, but if you find you do not get on with a particular brush stroke or you do not like part of the design, see 'Adapting design patterns' (page 39) for some alternative ideas.

You will be painting each design twice. First you will practise on acetate and, second, you will paint on the object. Unless you are an expert, it is important to practise first.

Order of work for each project

1 Practise the brush strokes listed for the project and be sure that you are familiar with the techniques before starting the project.

2 Your first step is to find an object to fit the project pattern. Each project has been done on a particular object. If you are a beginner, find a flat surface for your first piece as this is easier to work on than a curved surface. For beginners the object should not be too large – forget the milk churn that you always wanted to paint and leave this until you are familiar with all the brush strokes. Each project can, of course, be executed on any suitable object.

Certain projects in this book contain details of how to build the base object in wood. You can attempt these or ask a woodworker friend to help in their construction. When objects are difficult to find, there is often added satisfaction in making your own from start to finish, including decoration.

All the measurements are in inches followed by millimetre equivalents in brackets. On some of the shaped projects a grid of squares of 1 in (25 mm) is used on the drawings to indicate scale.

3 Prepare the object ready for background painting, but do not paint the background at this stage.

4 Trace the pattern from the book (each pattern is to be found within its project). Hold the tracing paper in place using masking tape or paper clips. Remove the tracing carefully. See 'Tracing and transferring a design pattern' (page 38) for further information.

5 Place a sheet of acetate over the top of the tracing and attach with masking tape.

6 Follow the instructions for painting the pattern by finding the brushes required and setting out your palette with the colours already mixed. Practise the whole of the pattern on acetate.

7 When the painting is complete, remove the acetate from the tracing.

8 If you wish to choose your own background, now is the time to decide on the colour. To help you choose, hold the acetate with the painted design over or next to various colour charts or cards.

9 Paint the background plain or use any of the various techniques for enhancing the background.

10 Trace the pattern on to the object.

11 You will notice in the painting instructions of each project that some of the colours should come straight from the tube but others need to be mixed. To help you recognize that a mixed colour has been used, the name of the colour starts with a small letter instead of a capital. Here are some examples:

- Hooker's Green (this colour is straight from the tube)
- *medium green*: Hooker's Green + touch Titanium White (this is a slightly lighter colour than Hooker's Green and therefore a little white needs to be added)
- *light green*: medium green + more Titanium White (this is a lighter shade than medium green and more white has been added)
- *peach*: Vermilion (Hue) + Titanium White + touch Cadmium Yellow

Note: The first colour is the main colour on your palette, the second colour should be added slowly to the first, then the 'touch ' should be added last.

12 Decorate the object according to the project instructions. You will notice in some projects that I stop painting one flower without finishing it and go on to paint something else. This is done for a reason. I have anticipated the fact that the paint in that particular area will not be sufficiently dry to add other strokes on top and I therefore return to that area at a later stage.

13 Protect your project, following the instructions on page 56.

14 Antique the finish if wished (see page 56) and then protect again.

FIG. 14 *Distribution of techniques among projects*

Projects	Basic brush strokes	Dots	Tipping	Double loading	Triple loading	Floating colour	Cross-hatching	Tendrils	Dry brushing	Sponge blending	Stippling	Basic crescent brush stroke	Dipped crescent brush stroke	Ruffled crescent brush stroke	Pointed crescent brush stroke	Jagged crescent brush stroke	Rose petal brush stroke	Sponge pollen effect
1 Blue and white flowers	•	•																•
2 Daisy bouquet	•	•	•															•
3 Canal ware roses	•	•	•			•												
4 Ukranian flowers	•	•	•															
5 Spinner's chair	•	•	•						•									•
6 Honeysuckle	•	•	•		•	•												
7 Spring flowers	•	•	•	•		•							•					•
8 Nasturtiums	•	•	•			•			•				•					
9 Strawberries	•	•	•			•		•		•								
10 Mixed fruit	•	•	•			•				•								
11 Bavarian flowers and bird	•	•	•	•								•						
12 Hinderlooper	•								•			•						
13 Fuchsia	•	•	•			•		•	•		•		•	•	•			
14 Sweet peas	•	•	•			•					•			•				
15 Poppies and corn	•	•	•	•		•												•
16 Rosemaling	•	•	•	•		•	•					•						
17 Clematis	•	•		•		•		•			•	•			•			
18 Roses	•	•	•	•		•											•	
19 Carnation spray	•	•	•	•		•										•		
20 Pennsylvania Dutch	•	•					•	•										

PROJECT 1
Blue and white flowers
....

This first design includes the comma and straight strokes. There is also an 'S' stroke in the border patterns. You will need to practise these brush strokes and dots before starting to paint the pattern. There is a choice of three borders which you can paint around the design.

The paddle shape was prepared as for bare wood and painted clay brown.

The style of the blue flower is characteristic of flowers found on Pennsylvania Dutch ware. The soft effect of the Queen Anne's lace is achieved by using a synthetic sponge.

I have painted comma strokes on top of the blue flower petals to add more depth to the design and added dots and comma strokes to fill in spaces.

There are only four main colours as you will be mixing your own shades of green and blue. Your colours may vary from those shown, but it will give your painting the personal touch.

Techniques
Basic brush strokes
Dots
Sponge pollen effect for flower centres

Brushes
D77 No. 6
D99 No. 1

Palette
Titanium White
Cadmium Yellow
Burnt Umber
Indanthrene Blue
medium blue: Indanthrene Blue + Titanium White
light blue: medium blue + touch more Titanium White
dark green: Indanthrene Blue + Cadmium Yellow
light green: dark green + touch Titanium White

Painting instructions

1 For all leaves, load the D77 No. 6 brush with dark green and paint single comma strokes for small leaves and two comma strokes for large leaves as shown in Fig. 15.

FIG. 15

2 You will need to turn your work around to paint the stalks. Load the D99 No. 1 brush with light green. Paint long comma strokes starting at the cut end of the stalk. Similarly paint comma strokes for veins on the leaves and overstrokes on the large leaves, as shown in the colour illustration.

3 For the ball flower, use a small piece of sponge placed in tweezers. Dip the sponge into light green paint, dab on to the palette to remove excess paint and gently dab a ball shape as shown in the colour illustration. Repeat lightly with Titanium White. Paint dots in Titanium White.

4 For the white daisy, load the D77 No. 6 brush with Titanium White. Paint four comma strokes and one straight stroke for the petals, varying the pressure on the brush and painting and finishing each petal in the centre, as shown in Fig. 16. (The brown centre will cover the tail ends of your brush strokes.) Paint the petals in numerical order.

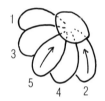

FIG. 16

When the petals have dried, load the D77 No. 6 brush with Burnt Umber and paint two comma strokes for the daisy centre (see Fig. 15). When dry, repeat the process so as to produce a denser colour.

Sponge the daisy centre with Cadmium Yellow for a pollen effect, using the sponge pollen technique. Continuing on the daisy centre, paint small dots in Cadmium Yellow using a cocktail stick.

5 For the darker blue flower, load the D77 No. 6 brush with medium blue and paint four comma strokes and one straight stroke for the petals, painting in numerical order as shown in Fig. 17.

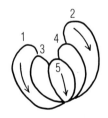

FIG. 17

6 For the pale blue flowers, load the D77 No. 6 brush with pale blue and paint comma strokes 1 to 4 in numerical order as shown in

Fig. 18. Reload the brush with medium blue and paint two comma strokes, 5 and 6, for the centre petals, using less pressure.

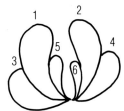

FIG. 18

7 For the pale blue bud, load the D77 No. 6 brush with pale blue and paint two comma and one straight strokes as shown in Fig. 19.

FIG. 19

8 Using the D99 No. 1 brush, follow the colour illustration for all blue flowers and paint comma and straight strokes on the petals. Paint the remaining comma and straight strokes according to the colour illustration.

9 Paint all the remaining dots in Titanium White and Cadmium Yellow using a brush handle. Paint the light green dots at the base of each blue flower with a brush handle.

Borders

Have fun with these or create your own variation. Starting from the top (see below right), this is how to paint them:

First border 'The line of life with its ups and downs', for which I used the D99 No. 1 brush. Think of the 'S' stroke when painting this line, varying the pressure through the curves.

Second border No brush is used for this, only a cocktail stick!

Third border A little more difficult. Using the D99 No. 1 brush, paint one 'S' stroke for the stalk and comma strokes for the leaves. Then paint four tiny comma strokes and one straight stroke for the petals.

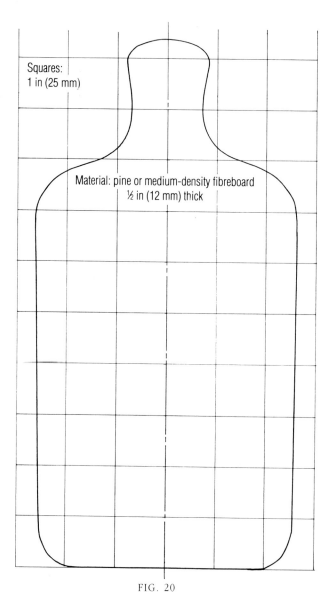

FIG. 20

Woodwork pattern for the paddle shape

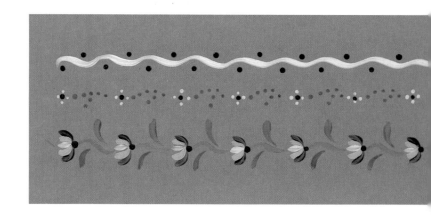

FIG. 21

PROJECT 2
Daisy bouquet
··············

The daisy bouquet consists of basic brush strokes only: the comma, straight and 'S' and 'C' strokes.

The waste-paper bin was prepared as for rusty metal and painted with a cream base coat. The spattering technique was used: the object was first spattered lightly with Permanent Violet and then with Yellow Ochre. These colours were chosen as they were used for the daisies.

A variety of colours was used for the daisies to illustrate the different effects that can be achieved by tipping a brush.

For the colour illustration white dots in groups of three have been painted around the bouquet, but on the waste-paper bin the dots have been omitted as they would be lost in the spattered background.

It is important to paint daisy petals in the numerical order indicated. This will ensure that each daisy does not finish up looking like a cartwheel. (Try painting the brush strokes in a clockwise direction to see what happens!)

Techniques
Basic brush strokes
Dots
Tipping
Sponge pollen effect
  for flower centres.

Brushes
D77 No. 6
D88 ⅜-in (10-mm)
D99 No. 1 liner

Palette
Titanium White
Cadmium Red Deep
Hooker's Green
Opaque Oxide of Chromium
Permanent Violet
Burnt Umber
light brown: Burnt Umber + Yellow Ochre
lilac: Titanium White + touch Permanent Violet
cream: Titanium White + touch Yellow Ochre
pink: Titanium White + touch Cadmium Red Deep

FIG. 22

Painting instructions

1 Instead of looking at the pattern the right way up, turn your work around so that the bow is away from you. This will ensure that you paint all the stalks in the right direction.

Load the No. 1 liner brush with Opaque Oxide of Chromium and tip with Titanium White. Paint four comma strokes and one straight stroke for the cut ends of the stalks which are now above the bow.

Keeping the work in the same position, paint the remaining stalks using comma and straight strokes, but without tipping the brush. Place the pattern the correct way up again.

2 For the daisy petals, load the D77 No. 6 brush with the appropriate colour (see the list below) and paint comma and straight strokes for the petals in numerical order as shown in Fig. 23. It is important to keep turning your work so that all the brush strokes are placed in the correct position.

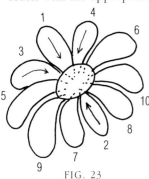

FIG. 23

A Paint the petals in pink.
B Paint the petals in pink tipped with Titanium White.
C Paint the first row of petals in pink and for the second row tip the brush with Cadmium Red Deep.
D Paint the first row of petals in pink and for the second row tip the brush with Titanium White.
E Paint the petals in cream tipped with Yellow Ochre.
F Paint the first row of petals in cream and for the second row tip the brush with Yellow Ochre.
G Paint the petals in lilac tipped with Permanent Violet.

3 For the daisy centres, load the D77 No. 6 brush with light brown and paint the flower centres using two comma strokes, as shown in Fig. 24.

Allow to dry and repeat the process so as to produce a denser colour.

Using the sponge pollen technique for the flower centres, sponge first with cream and then Titanium White.

Load the No. 1 liner brush with light brown and paint a comma stroke at the base of each flower centre.

Paint dots for the stamens in Burnt Umber using a cocktail stick.

4 For the buds, load the D77 No. 6 brush with cream and tip with Yellow Ochre. Paint three straight strokes at the back of each bud (see Fig. 25). Follow the numerical order indicated. Load the brush with cream tipped with Titanium White and paint two comma strokes and two straight strokes for the front petals as shown in Fig. 25.

For the sepals, load the D77 No. 6 brush with Opaque Oxide of Chromium and tip lightly with Hooker's Green. Reverse your work and paint two comma strokes, 8 and 9.

5 For the leaves, load the D88 ⅜-in (10-mm) brush with Opaque Oxide of Chromium and tip lightly with Hooker's Green. Paint all the large leaves with 'S' strokes, painting each from the centre of the bouquet outwards.

Load the D77 No. 6 brush with Opaque Oxide of Chromium and tip lightly with Hooker's Green. Paint all the comma stroke leaves.

6 For the ribbon, follow the numerical order in Fig. 26 when painting the bow. For all the brush strokes, load the D88 ⅜-in (10-mm) brush with lilac tipped with Permanent Violet.

For the loops of the bow, paint sweeping 'C' strokes in the direction shown. For each part of the streamers, paint an 'S' stroke – four in all.

For the knot, paint one 'C' stroke.

7 Paint the white dots with a brush handle.

FIG. 24

FIG. 25

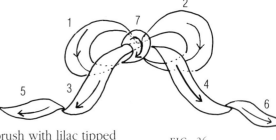

FIG. 26

PROJECT 3
Canal ware roses
••••••••••••••••

There are various forms of canal roses. I have chosen a simple rose for this project.

The jug (page 70) was prepared as for rusty metal and then painted red. Traditional backgrounds are black, red, blue and green, with black being the favourite colour.

If you are painting larger roses, use larger brushes for the petals – that is, D77 Nos 6 and 8.

Techniques
Basic brush strokes
Dots
Floating colour

Brushes
D88 ¼-in (6-mm) and ⅜-in (10-mm)
D77 No. 3 and 6
D99 No. 1

Palette
Cadmium Yellow Deep
Cadmium Yellow
Titanium White
Payne's Grey
Burnt Sienna
pink: Titanium White + touch Cadmium Red Deep
dark pink: pink + touch more Cadmium Red Deep
red: Cadmium Red Deep + Vermilion (Hue)
dark red: red + touch Payne's Grey
dark brown: dark red + touch more Payne's Grey
orange: Vermilion (Hue) + Cadmium Yellow Deep
green: Monestial Turquoise + Cadmium Yellow Deep

FIG. 27

FIG. 28

STEP-BY-STEP GUIDE TO PAINTING CANAL WARE ROSES

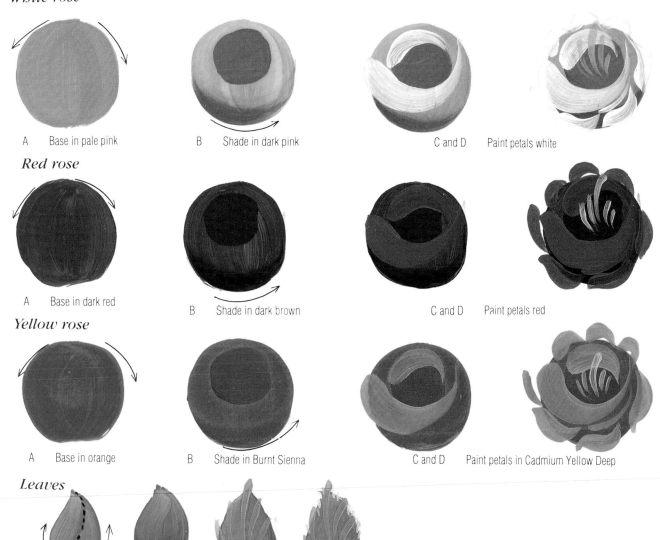

White rose

A   Base in pale pink   B   Shade in dark pink   C and D   Paint petals white

Red rose

A   Base in dark red   B   Shade in dark brown   C and D   Paint petals red

Yellow rose

A   Base in orange   B   Shade in Burnt Sienna   C and D   Paint petals in Cadmium Yellow Deep

Leaves

A   B   C   D

Painting instructions

Follow the steps in the colour illustration (page 69) in conjunction with the instructions below.

1 For the leaves:

A Load the D88 ¼-in (6-mm) brush with green and paint one comma and one 'S' stroke for each leaf.

B Load the D88 ⅜-in (10-mm) brush with Burnt Sienna as for floating colour and paint shading at the base of each leaf using a 'C' stroke.

C Load the D99 No. 1 brush with Cadmium Yellow Deep and paint comma strokes.

D Load the D99 No. 1 brush with Titanium White and paint tiny, white, straight strokes.

2 For the basic rose, follow the colour illustration for the different colour build-up of each bloom:

A Load the D88 ¼-in (6-mm) brush with your chosen colour and fill in a circle, following the shape, with 'C' strokes.

B Load the D88 ¼-in (6-mm) brush and paint 'C' strokes to form the centre shading. Load the D88 ⅜-in (10-mm) brush as for floating colour and paint a 'C' stroke at the base of the rose.

C Load the D77 No. 6 brush and paint two comma strokes.

D Load the D77 No. 3 brush and paint the brush strokes shown, apart from two small petal strokes – for the latter, use the D99 No. 1 brush. Note that the bottom petals are slightly 'S' shaped. For stamens, load the D99 No. 1 brush with Cadmium Yellow and paint comma strokes.

3 Load the D99 No. 1 brush with Cadmium Yellow Deep and paint long comma strokes, following the colour illustration.

4 Paint the white dots using a brush handle.

PROJECT 4
Ukrainian flowers
• • • • • • • • • • • • • • •

I chose an old flat iron for this small group of Ukrainian flowers.

There are five borders for you to paint, all consisting of basic brush strokes: one floral border around the group of flowers and four traditional borders in gold. For the floral border, follow the painting instructions for individual flowers and leaves in the main central group.

The iron (page 73) was prepared as for rusty metal and painted black. When decorating an object which is an awkward shape, such as an iron, take care to set it in a stable position before painting.

Gold paint was used to tip the brush when painting the leaves on the iron, but for the colour illustration the brush was tipped with Cadmium Yellow. In the following instructions, reference is made to the iron when Gold is given in brackets following another colour.

FIG. 29

Painting instructions

1 For the circular yellow flower, load the D77 No. 3 brush with Cadmium Yellow Deep and tip with Cadmium Yellow. Paint two straight strokes for each petal as shown in Fig. 30.

FIG. 30

Load the No. 0 liner brush with Payne's Grey and paint two tiny comma strokes and one straight stroke at the base of each petal starting at the tip end.

Load the eraser on end of a pencil (or the handle of the D77 No. 3 brush) with Cadmium Yellow Deep and paint the centre of the flower.

2 For the yellow-tipped flower, load the D77 No. 6 brush with Vermilion (Hue) tipped with Cadmium Yellow Deep (Gold) and paint the petals in numerical order, as shown in Fig. 31. The first petal is painted as an 'S' stroke but with pressure at the beginning of the stroke.

FIG. 31

3 For the Vermilion-tipped flower, load the D77 No. 6 brush with Cadmium Red Deep and tip with Vermilion (Hue) and paint as in step 2 above.

4 Paint Payne's Grey dots at the base of the flowers of steps 2 and 3 above. Load the No. 0 liner brush with Payne's Grey and paint brush strokes from the dot into each petal.

5 For the red berries, paint Cadmium Red Deep dots in descending order of size. Then, when dry, paint Cadmium Yellow Deep (Gold) dots to one side of the red dot, also in descending order.

6 For the heart, load the D88 ⅜-in (10-mm) brush with blood red and paint one straight stroke in the centre of the heart starting from point X, and one comma stroke on either side, again commencing at point X, as shown in Fig. 32.

FIG. 32

Techniques
Basic brush strokes
Dots
Tipping

Brushes
D77 Nos 3 and 6
D88 ⅜-in (10-mm)
D99 Nos 1 and 3
No. 0 liner

Palette
Cadmium Yellow
Cadmium Yellow Deep (Gold)
Vermilion (Hue)
Cadmium Red Deep
Payne's Grey
blood red: Cadmium Red + Vermilion (Hue)
dark green: Hooker's Green + touch Titanium White

Allow to dry and repeat the process so as to produce a denser colour.

Load the D99 No. 3 brush with Vermilion (Hue) tipped with Cadmium Yellow Deep (Gold) and paint four comma strokes on the heart.

Load the D99 No. 1 brush with Vermilion (Hue) (Gold) and paint two 'S' strokes at the base of the heart.

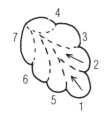

FIG. 33

7 For the two large leaves, load the D77 No. 3 brush with dark green and tip with Cadmium Yellow (Gold). Paint straight and comma strokes in numerical order, as shown in Fig. 33.

Load the No. 0 liner brush with Payne's Grey and paint a vein through the centre of the large leaves, starting at the stalk end. When dry, paint Cadmium Yellow Deep (Gold) dots in descending order on the top of the vein.

Paint the remaining leaves: load the D77 No. 3 brush with dark green tipped with Cadmium Yellow Deep (Gold) and paint comma strokes.

8 Load the D99 No. 1 brush with dark green and paint the stalks.

9 For the final details, paint comma and straight strokes above the red flowers by loading the No. 0 liner brush with Cadmium Yellow Deep (Gold).

Paint the remaining dots by following the colour illustration.

Traditional borders

All four borders were painted using the No. 0 liner brush and the dots were painted with a cocktail stick.

The four gold borders are all based on the 'S' stroke. The second border is the same as the first, but has been embellished with extra brush strokes.

Practise the borders by placing a sheet of acetate over the top, as for basic brush strokes.

The flowers in the floral border are miniatures of the main pattern. Use the D77 No. 3 brush for the petals and leaves. Use the No. 0 Liner brush for all other brush strokes.

PROJECT 5
Spinner's chair
•••••••••••

in this pattern, so it is necessary to mix the paint to the correct consistency.

To extend the pattern for the back of the chair, trace the pattern, repeating the order of the daisies until there are five open flowers in a consecutive line above the ribbon.

This chair was made using pine wood and prepared as for bare wood. It was stained with an acrylic wash made from a mixture of colours: Yellow Ochre + touch Burnt Umber + touch Hooker's Green.

The design is adapted from Bavarian style. I have not used the traditional bright colours of Bavarian painting but toned the colours to match the colour wash of the chair. For example, Burnt Umber, Yellow Ochre and Opaque Oxide of Chromium have been used as basic colours. Vermilion (Hue) and Titanium White help provide the wide range of subtle shades.

With traditional Bavarian painting the brush is just wiped and not washed when painting one particular flower or leaf. You can try the Bavarian method or, if you prefer, wash your brush when loading it with a new colour.

There is a considerable amount of line work

Back

FIG. 34

Seat

FIG. 35

Painting instructions for the chair seat

1 Paint all the leaves in medium green as follows:

For the four large leaves, load the D88 ⅜-in (10-mm) brush and paint two comma strokes and one 'S' stroke, as shown in Fig. 36.

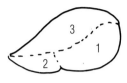

FIG. 36

For the remaining small leaves, load the D77 No. 3 brush and paint with comma or 'S' strokes.

2 Repeat step 1 above if the background colour shows through the large leaves.

3 For the line work on all leaves, load the D99 No. 1 brush with the appropriate colour and follow the colour illustration.

For the four large leaves, load the brush with white and paint an 'S' stroke with pressure on the brush at the beginning of the stroke, starting at the tip of the leaf.

Load the brush with dark green and paint comma strokes.

Techniques
Basic brush strokes
Dots
Tipping
Dry brushing
Sponge pollen effect for flower centres

Brushes
D77 Nos 3 and 6
D88 ¼-in (6-mm) and ⅜-in (10-mm)
D99 Nos 1 and 3

Palette
Burnt Umber
Yellow Ochre
Titanium White
medium green: Opaque Oxide of Chromium + touch Yellow Ochre
dark green: medium green + Hooker's Green
apricot: Yellow Ochre + Vermilion (Hue) + Titanium White
peach: apricot + more Titanium White
cream: Titanium White + Yellow Ochre

For the small leaves, load the brush with Titanium White and paint 'S' and comma strokes on the leaves.

Load the D99 No. 1 brush with dark green and paint all the comma and 'S' strokes.

4 Load the No. 1 liner brush with dark green and paint flowing strokes for the stalks, starting from the cut end of the flowers and continuing into the leaves where necessary.

5 Load the D77 No. 3 brush with Titanium White and paint the bell flowers with back-to-back comma strokes.

6 For the large, gold, double daisy, load the D77 No. 6 brush with cream and tip with Yellow Ochre. Paint the petals in numerical order, as shown in Project 1, step 4.

7 Load the D77 No. 3 brush as in step 6 above and continue working wet-on-wet. Paint another row of shorter petals on top of the first row.

8 For the remaining single daisies, load the D77 No. 3 brush and paint as in step 6 above.

9 Paint all the chrysanthemums *one at a time.* For the two large and one medium flowers, load the D88 ⅜-in (10-mm) brush with apricot and paint one 'C' stroke across the top of the flower, as shown in Fig. 37.

FIG. 37

10 Load the D77 No. 6 brush with apricot and tip with peach. Paint the petals in numerical order, covering the lower edge of the 'C' stroke, as in shown in Fig. 38.

11 For smaller chrysanthemums use the same colours but load the D88 ¼-in (6-mm) brush for the 'C' stroke and the D77 No. 3 for the petals.

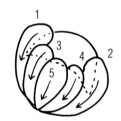

FIG. 38

12 Paint the flat, round, apricot daisies one at a time so that you are working wet-on-wet. Load the D77 No. 3 brush with apricot and tip with peach. Paint the base row of petals using straight strokes in numerical order, as shown in Fig. 39. Paint a second row of petals placed in between the first row.

13 Paint the centres of the gold daisies with

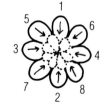

FIG. 39

Burnt Umber using the dry brush technique and the D77 No. 3 brush.

14 Sponge the daisy centres with cream using the sponge pollen technique.

15 Paint all dots and white comma strokes according to the colour illustration.

Painting instructions for the chair back

1 Paint the leaves as for the chair seat, but use the D77 No. 6 brush.

2 Load the D99 No. 3 brush with medium green and paint comma and straight strokes for all the stalks.

3 Load the D99 No. 1 brush with Titanium White and paint a straight stroke on the central stalks.

4 Paint the large, gold daisy as for the chair seat.

5 Paint the round, flat, apricot daisy as for the chair seat.

6 Paint the ribbon with the D88 ⅜-in (10-mm) brush loaded with peach and tipped with apricot. Paint one 'C' stroke for the knot and four 'S' strokes for the streamers as in Project 2, step 6.

7 Paint all dots.

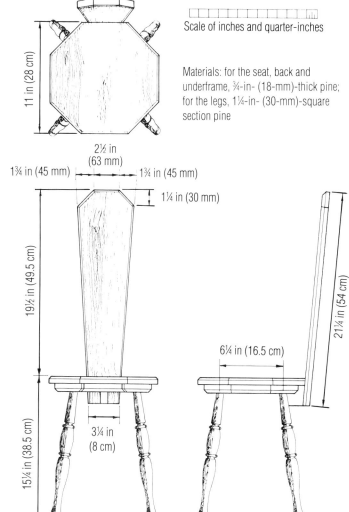

Scale of inches and quarter-inches

Materials: for the seat, back and underframe, ¾-in- (18-mm)-thick pine; for the legs, 1¼-in- (30-mm)-square section pine

FIG. 40
Woodwork pattern for the spinner's chair

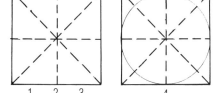
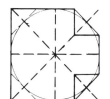

1 2 3   4

5   The octagon

Fig. 41 *Drawing an octagon*

The octagon (eight-sided shape), as used for the seat of the spinner's chair, is often needed as a clock face, as a box, or as a table decoration. An easy and perfectly accurate way to draw the shape is as follows:

1 Cut a square piece of paper with each side the same length as the distance from side to side of the octagon. In the case of the chair, the side of the square will be 11 in (28 cm).
2 Fold the paper from corner to corner in both directions and then lay it flat.
3 Fold the paper from side to side in both directions and then lay it flat. You now have a square with four folds passing through the centre point.
4 Draw a circle from the centre point to touch all four sides. In the case of the chair, the circle will have a 5 ½-in (14-cm) radius.
5 At each corner, fold the paper over as shown. Cut off the corners, and the shape is ready. It is useful to transfer the shape on to card or thin board so that you can use it again.

PROJECT 6
Honeysuckle
·········

Techniques
Basic brush strokes
Tipping
Triple loading
Floating colour

Brushes
D77 No. 3
D88 ¼-in (6-mm) and ⅜-in (10-mm)
D99 Nos. 1 and 3
No. 0 liner

Palette
Titanium White
Hooker's Green
medium green: Hooker's Green + touch Cadmium
 Yellow + touch Titanium White
light green: medium green + touch more Titanium
 White
cream: Titanium White + touch Cadmium Yellow
burgundy: Permanent Rose + touch Payne's Grey

The garden honeysuckle is ideal for practising those comma strokes! Triple loading the brush for the uppermost petal gives the lovely blend of colour required for this petal.

The honeysuckle pattern has been painted on a house number sign (page 82). The wooden sign was prepared as for bare wood and then varnished with exterior varnish.

FIG. 42

Painting instructions

Note: There are two No. 3 brushes used in this pattern, so make sure that you have the correct brush in hand.

1 Load the D88 ¼-in (6-mm) brush with medium green and undercoat the leaves, using one comma and one 'S' stroke, as shown in Project 3, step 1A. Larger leaves may need the D88 ⅜-in (10-mm) brush. When dry, paint the top coat.

2 For the stalks, load the No. 0 liner brush with light green tipped with burgundy. Paint two long comma strokes, starting from either side of the main group of flowers.

3 For the leaf veins, load the No. 0 liner brush with light green lightly tipped with burgundy and paint flowing comma strokes into the four leaves on either side of the centre group of flowers. Paint the remaining leaf veins with light green only, as shown in the colour illustration.

4 Load the No. 0 liner brush with light green and add curled edges to the leaves, starting at the tip end, by painting either comma or 'S' strokes, as shown in Fig. 43.

FIG. 43

FIG. 44

5 Load the D88 ⅜-in (10-mm) brush with Hooker's Green as for floating colour. Place the paint side of the brush *next* to the curl of the leaf, starting at the stalk end and following the outline, as shown in Fig. 44.

6 For the uppermost petal of each honeysuckle flower, triple load the D88 ¼-in (6-mm) brush with burgundy as the main colour and Titanium White on either side. Paint one comma stroke, as shown in Fig. 45. Reload the brush without washing for each petal and paint all the uppermost flower petals.

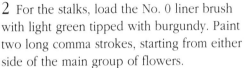

FIG. 45

For the lower petal, load the D99 No. 3 brush with cream and lightly dip the tip of the brush into burgundy. Paint a comma stroke, as shown in Fig. 45.

Working on the back of the uppermost petal, load the D99 No. 1 brush with burgundy. Make a long, flattened 'C' stroke, as shown in Fig. 46.

FIG. 46

7 For the buds, load the D77 No. 3 brush with burgundy and paint various-sized comma strokes.

8 Now paint the stamens. For the filaments (the long, stalk-like parts of the stamens), load the No. 0 liner brush with Titanium White. The filaments need to be fine, so it is necessary to stroke the brush on the wet palette once or twice before painting the first one, then paint in the direction shown in Fig. 47. Load the No. 0 liner brush with cream and paint the anthers (the pollen containers on the end of the filaments) as indicated in Fig. 47.

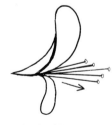

FIG. 47

PROJECT 7
Spring flowers
·············

Bluebells and primroses are much-favoured English flowers and both can easily be adapted for decorative folk painting.

The watering can was prepared as for rusty metal and painted light blue. The outside edges of the can were sprayed with a darker shade of blue as for sprayed borders.

Painting instructions

1 Load the D88 ⅜-in (10-mm) brush with Opaque Oxide of Chromium and paint all the primrose leaves, as in Project 5, step 1.

2 Load the D88 ¼-in (6-mm) brush with leaf green and dip into Hooker's Green, and paint all the remaining large leaves using 'S' and comma strokes, starting the stroke at the base of each leaf.

3 Load the D77 No. 3 brush with leaf green and paint straight and comma strokes for the remaining small leaves.

Techniques
Basic brush strokes
Dots
Tipping
Double loading
Floating colour
Tendrils
Closed dipped crescent
Sponge pollen effect for flower centres

Brushes
D77 No. 3
D88 ¼-in (6-mm) and ⅜-in (10-mm)
No. 0 liner

Palette
Cadmium Yellow
Cadmium Yellow Deep
Yellow Ochre
Titanium White
Hooker's Green
Opaque Oxide of Chromium
light green: Opaque Oxide of Chromium + touch Titanium White
leaf green: Opaque Oxide of Chrome + Cadmium Yellow (lightly mixed)
blue: Indanthrene Blue + Titanium White
orange: Cadmium Yellow Deep + touch Vermilion (Hue)
primrose: Cadmium Yellow + Titanium White

FIG. 49

FIG. 50

4 Load the D77 No. 3 brush with Titanium White and paint the daisy petals in numerical order, as shown in Project 2, step 2.

5 Dab a piece of fine sponge into Cadmium Yellow and light green and lightly sponge all four large leaves to give a little texture.

6 Double load the D88 ⅜-in (10-mm) brush with primrose and Cadmium Yellow Deep and paint five closed dipped crescent brush strokes, as shown in Fig. 49, with the primrose colour leading.

7 Paint the buds in same manner, as shown in Fig. 50.

8 Load the D77 No. 3 brush with leaf green and paint two comma strokes underneath the primrose buds, as shown in Fig. 50.

9 Load the No. 0 liner brush with light green and paint all the scrolls, veins, grasses and the bottom edge on the primrose leaves.

10 Load the No. 0 liner brush with Hooker's Green and paint the remaining stalks, and a few random veins on the leaves.

11 Load the D77 No. 3 brush with blue and paint the bluebells using one

FIG. 51

FIG. 48

straight stroke and two comma strokes, as shown in Fig. 51. Paint the bluebell buds with the brush tipped with Titanium White.

12 For the daisy centres, load the D88 ¼-in (6-mm) brush with Cadmium Yellow Deep and paint two comma strokes. If necessary, repeat when dry to produce a denser colour.

13 Sponge the daisy centres with primrose using the sponge pollen technique.

14 Load a sponge lightly with light green and Titanium White and dab around the grass stalks, as shown in the colour illustration.

15 Load the No. 0 liner brush with Yellow Ochre and paint a 'C' stroke on the underside of each daisy centre.

16 Using a cocktail stick, paint all the Titanium White dots.

17 Paint an orange dot for each primrose centre.

18 Load the D88 ⅜-in (10-mm) brush with Hooker's Green as for floating colour and shade the four large leaves as in Project 6, step 5.

PROJECT 8
Nasturtiums
········

Nasturtiums are forgotten flowers when it comes to decorative painting, yet their brilliant orange and yellow colours can add a touch of summer to any room.

The shelf (page 89) was prepared as for bare wood and painted cream. It was antiqued using the antiquing-before-decoration technique. The colours used for antiquing were Burnt Sienna and Yellow Ochre.

To trace the pattern, trace the right-hand side first, then reverse the pattern, folding it in half on the broken line. Trace the lines for the left-hand side.

Note: It is advisable to undercoat all nasturtium flowers in Titanium White when painting on a dark background.

Techniques

Basic brush strokes
Dots
Floating colour
Dry brushing
Dipped crescent

Brushes

D77 No. 3
D88 ¼-in (6-mm) and ⅜-in (10-mm)
D99 No. 1

Palette

Burnt Sienna
Cadmium Red Deep
Cadmium Orange
Cadmium Yellow
Cadmium Yellow Deep
Yellow Ochre
Hooker's Green
Opaque Oxide of Chromium
light green: Opaque Oxide of Chromium + Titanium
   White
cream: Titanium White + touch Cadmium Yellow
   Deep

FIG. 52

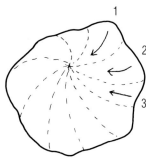

FIG. 53

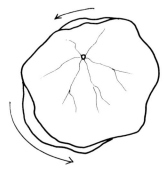

FIG. 54

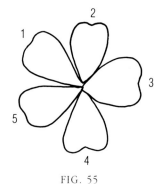

FIG. 55

Painting instructions

1 Paint all the leaves in Opaque Oxide of Chromium as follows:

For the large leaves, load the D88 ⅜-in (10-mm) brush and paint comma strokes working in a clockwise direction, until the entire leaf is filled, as shown in Fig. 53.

For the small leaves, load the D88 ¼-in (6-mm) brush and paint as for the large leaves (above).

When dry, repeat the process for both large and small leaves to produce a denser colour.

2 For all leaves:

Load the D99 No. 1 brush with light green and paint the leaf turns using long, misshapen 'C' strokes, as shown in Fig. 54.

Paint one light green dot in the centre of each leaf. Load the D99 No. 1 brush with light green and paint veins working from the centre dot outwards, as shown in Fig. 54.

Paint shadows on the leaves by loading the D88 ⅜-in (10-mm) brush with Hooker's Green as for floating colour. Shade with Hooker's Green next to the turn of the leaf, as in Project 6, step 5.

Load the D99 No. 1 brush with light green and paint long, flowing stalks to join the leaves and flowers together.

3 For the three orange nasturtium flowers and buds, load the D88 ⅜-in (10-mm) brush with Cadmium Orange and paint using a closed dipped crescent brush stroke for each petal. Do not overlap the petals: see Fig. 55. The large nasturtium will require more pressure on the brush. Fill in any gap in the centre.

Repeat the above process using Cadmium

Yellow Deep for the remaining nasturtium flowers and buds.

For the centre of all the open nasturtiums, load the D88 ⅜-in (10-mm) brush with Burnt Sienna as for floating colour and paint one 'C' stroke in the centre of each flower, as shown in Fig. 56.

For all open orange nasturtiums, load a dry brush with Cadmium Yellow Deep and dry

FIG. 56

brush the paint from the outside of the 'C', stroking the paint towards the edge of the petals, as shown in the colour illustration.

Dry brush the Cadmium Yellow Deep nasturtium using Cadmium Red Deep colour.

Load the D88 ⅜-in (10-mm) brush with Cadmium Yellow as for floating colour and highlight the outside edge of all the open orange nasturtium petals as shown in the colour illustration.

Repeat the highlight using cream for all the open yellow nasturtiums.

Load the D99 No. 1 brush with Yellow Ochre and paint one straight stroke for the pistil in the centre of each open flower.

4 Load the D77 No. 3 brush with Opaque Oxide of Chromium and paint 'S' and comma strokes for sepals on all the buds as shown in the colour illustration.

5 Paint cream dots for all stamens and an Opaque Oxide of Chromium dot at the base of each sepal.

This diagram shows half the shape for the back of the shelf unit.
The squares are 1 in (25 mm).
The shelf itself can be made as wide as you like.
The example in Project 8 is 4 in (10 cm) wide.

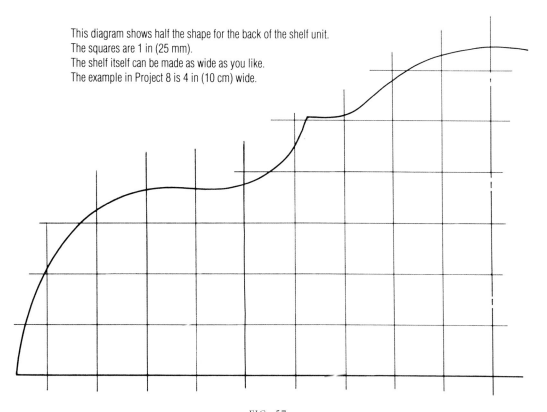

FIG. 57
Woodwork pattern for the shelf

PROJECT 9
Strawberries
....

No folk art book would be complete without strawberries, and in this project they have been painted on a stool (page 91) which was antiqued after decoration.

The pine wood was prepared as for bare wood and then stained medium oak. This colour provides a natural background for antiquing.

After the final decoration, the stool was antiqued using Burnt Umber oil paint. It was varnished both before and after decoration with an oil-based polyurethane varnish.

You will notice in the palette instructions that I have added a touch of Burnt Umber paint to obtain medium green for the leaves, to help tone the green with the medium oak background. When using other background colours, omit the Burnt Umber from the green.

Techniques
Basic brush strokes
Dots
Tipping
Floating colour
Tendrils
Sponge blending

Brushes
D88 ¼-in (6-mm) and ⅜-in (10-mm)
D77 No. 3
D99 No. 1

Palette
Burnt Umber
Titanium White
Burnt Sienna
Hooker's Green
Cadmium Yellow Deep
Cadmium Yellow
Payne's Grey
Vermilion (Hue)
Cadmium Red Deep
medium green: Hooker's Green + Titanium White + touch Burnt Umber
blackberry: Permanent Violet + Burnt Umber + touch Titanium White

Painting instructions

1 For the small leaves, load the D88 ¼-in (6-mm) brush with medium green and paint comma and straight strokes where appropriate.

For the large leaves, load the D88 ¼-in (6-mm) brush with medium green and paint one 'S' and one comma stroke, as in Project 3, step 1A.

2 For the leaf stalks, load the D99 No. 1 brush with Hooker's Green and paint flowing strokes, continuing each stroke into each leaf to form a central vein. Paint the remaining leaf veins on the five large leaves.

3 Load the D88 ¼-in (6-mm) brush with Cadmium Yellow and undercoat the strawberries using comma strokes, as shown in Fig. 58.

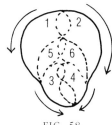

FIG. 58

4 When dry, repeat step 3 if painting on a dark background.

5 Paint the blossom petals by loading the D88 ¼-in (6-mm) brush with Titanium White. Paint two straight strokes for each petal as shown in Fig. 59. You will need to do this carefully on the two daisies either side of the central daisy.

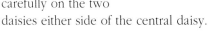

FIG. 59

6 When dry, paint the centre of each blossom. Load the D88 ¼-in (6-mm) brush with Cadmium Yellow Deep and paint 'C' strokes until the flower centre is filled in.

7 When dry, repeat step 6 to produce a denser colour.

8 Continue painting the strawberries, one at a time, using the sponge blending technique. Load the D88 ¼-in (6-mm) brush with Cadmium Red Deep and paint four comma strokes in numerical order on the outside of each strawberry as shown in Fig. 60.

9 Wipe the brush and generously load with Vermilion (Hue), filling in the centre of each strawberry, as shown in Fig. 61, and sponge blend.

10 Highlight the strawberries by painting Cadmium Yellow dots as shown in Fig. 62.

11 Load the D99 No. 1 brush with Cadmium Red Deep and outline the strawberries.

12 Load the D88 ¼-in (6-mm) brush with blackberry and paint two tiny 'C' strokes for each berry (you can also use an eraser at the end of a pencil, using the dot technique).

13 To highlight the berries, load a tiny piece of sponge with a touch of Titanium White and pat each berry once.

14 Paint a dot in Payne's Grey at the end of each berry. To highlight the berries further,

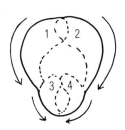

FIG. 60

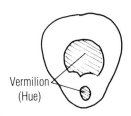

Vermilion (Hue)

FIG. 61

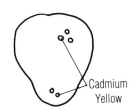

Cadmium Yellow

FIG. 62

FIG. 63

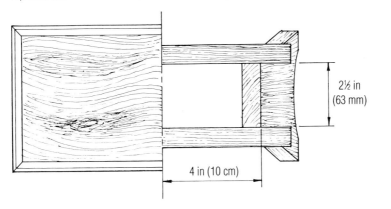

FIG. 64

paint another dot using Titanium White with a touch of blackberry colour added.

15 Load the D77 No. 3 brush with medium green tipped with Hooker's Green and paint the strawberry sepals in numerical order as shown in Fig. 64.

16 Add seeds to the strawberries by loading the D99 No. 1 brush with Burnt Umber. Paint tiny straight and comma strokes on the strawberries and add Cadmium Yellow Deep dots (using a cocktail stick) next to these brown brush strokes, as shown in the colour illustration.

17 Load the D99 No. 1 brush with Burnt Sienna and paint two comma strokes on the outside of each blossom petal. Paint two 'C' strokes in each blossom centre.

18 Load the D88 ⅜-in (10-mm) brush with Hooker's Green as for floating colour and shade the base of all the smaller leaves using variously sized 'C' strokes. For the five large leaves, shade following the outside edge of the central flower petals.

19 Load the D99 No. 1 brush with medium green and paint the tendrils and scrolls. Continue by painting the strawberry stalks, starting from the sepals on the top of each fruit.

Top view, drawn with half the top removed to show leg and rail detail

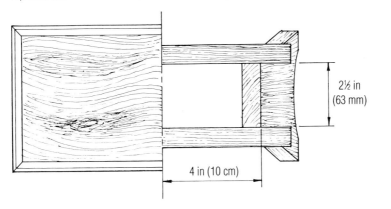

2½ in (63 mm)

4 in (10 cm)

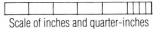

Scale of inches and quarter-inches

Material: for all parts, pine ¾ in (18 mm) thick

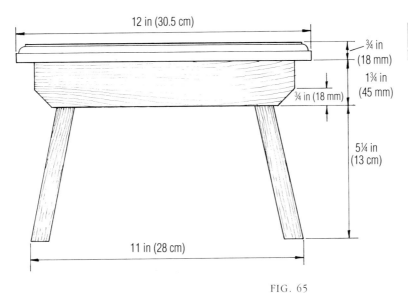

12 in (30.5 cm)

¾ in (18 mm)

1¾ in (45 mm)

¾ in (18 mm)

5¼ in (13 cm)

11 in (28 cm)

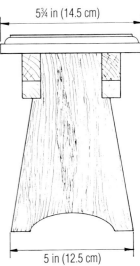

5¾ in (14.5 cm)

5 in (12.5 cm)

FIG. 65
Woodwork pattern for the stool

PROJECT 10
Mixed fruit
......

$\mathbf{F}$ruit is, and always will be, a favourite subject of the decorative folk artist. The sponge blending method of painting textured fruit, such as oranges and peaches, makes it much simpler to achieve the desired effect.

The wooden tray was prepared as for bare wood and painted dark green. The sides of the tray were then sprayed with gold to give relief from the expanse of green. Stained wood is also a good background colour for these fruits.

FIG. 66

STEP-BY-STEP GUIDE TO SPONGE BLENDING FRUIT

Oranges

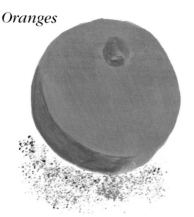  

Base whole of orange in Cadmium Orange.
Shade with Burnt Sienna.

Sponge blend.
Paint highlight in Titanium White.

Sponge blend.
Paint comma strokes in Opaque Oxide of Chromium.

Peaches

Do not blend this edge

Base whole of peach in Cadmium Yellow Deep.
Shade base of peach with Burnt Sienna.
Paint ripeness in Cadmium Red Deep.

Sponge blend, being careful not to blend in crease line.
Paint highlight in Titanium White.

Sponge blend: Paint thin line in Cadmium Red Deep on crease line.
Paint stalk Burnt Umber.

Apricots

Do not blend this edge

Base whole of apricot in Cadmium Orange.
Shade in Burnt Sienna.
Highlight in Cadmium Yellow Deep.

Sponge blend, being careful not to blend in crease line.
Paint highlight in Titanium White.

Sponge blend. Paint thin line in Cadmium Red Deep on crease line.
Paint stalk Burnt Umber.

Grapes

Base in black grape. Highlight in Titanium White.
Sponge blend.

Base in green grape. Highlight in Titanium White and Cadmium Yellow. Sponge blend.

Painting instructions

Follow the painting instructions in conjunction with the steps in the colour illustration.

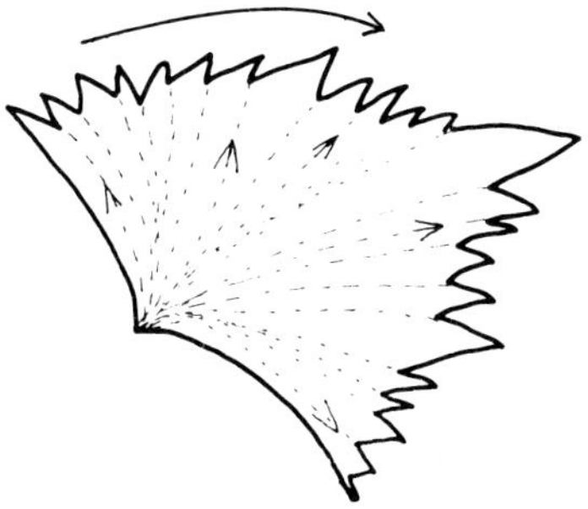

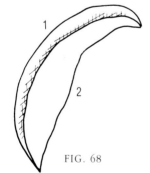

FIG. 67

1 Load the D77 No. 6 brush with Opaque Oxide of Chromium and paint the vine leaves using comma and straight strokes and working anti-clockwise, as shown in Fig. 67. All brush strokes start at the point where the stalk joins the leaf.

2 Load the D99 No. 1 brush with Hooker's Green and paint the vine leaf veins and short straight strokes to outline the vine leaf.

3 Load the D88 ⅜-in (10-mm) brush with white and undercoat all the fruit, following the contours with 'C' strokes.

4 For the fruit, follow the step-by-step guide to sponge blending fruit in the colour illustration, starting with the orange. Each fruit

Techniques
Basic brush strokes
Dots
Tipping
Floating colour
Sponge blending

Brushes
D77 Nos 3 and 6
D88 ¼-in (6-mm) and ⅜-in (10-mm)
D99 No. 1

Palette
Cadmium Orange
Cadmium Yellow Deep
Cadmium Yellow
Cadmium Red Deep
Vermilion (Hue)
Burnt Umber
Titanium White
Hooker's Green
Opaque Oxide of Chromium
brown: Burnt Sienna + Yellow Ochre
black grape: Permanent Violet + touch Payne's Grey
green grape: Opaque Oxide of Chromium + touch Cadmium Yellow

should be painted as a whole and then any fruit in front of it in the pattern will be painted on top. You will need to use the D88 ⅜-in (10-mm) brush for the base colour and the D88 ¼-in (6-mm) brush for shading and highlighting. The D88 ¼-in (6-mm) brush only is required for grapes. For stalks and liner work, use the D99 No. 1 brush.

5 Paint the strawberries according to the instructions for Project 9, steps 3, 8, 9, 10, 11, 15 and 16.

6 For the leaves on the orange, load the D88 ¼-in (6-mm) brush with green grape. Paint the right-hand leaf with one comma and one 'S' stroke; paint the left-hand leaf with two open 'C' strokes overlapping each other, as indicated in Fig. 68.

7 Load the D99 No. 1 brush with Opaque Oxide of Chromium and add veins to the orange leaves.

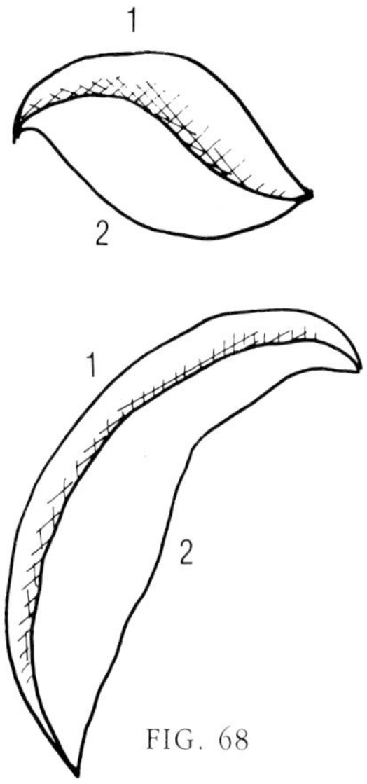

8 When dry, add shading to the leaves: load D88 ⅜-in (10-mm) brush with Hooker's Green as for floating colour and paint the shade line as indicated in Fig. 68.

FIG. 68

9 For shading between the fruit, load the D88 ⅜-in (10-mm) brush with brown and floating colour and add shading as shown in the colour photograph.

10 Load the D77 No. 6 brush with Burnt Umber and paint one long comma stroke for each grape stalk.

11 Continuing with the stalks, load the D99 No. 1 brush with Titanium White and paint lines on the stalks, as shown in the colour photograph.

PROJECT 11
Bavarian flowers and bird
·········

The traditional-style tulips and roses are fun to paint and consist of basic brush strokes.

The milk can was prepared as for non-rusty metal and painted green. I have designed this pattern using only basic brush strokes as the milk can would be too heavy to move around when painting a design using more difficult strokes. It is generally easier to chose a pattern with basic brush strokes when working on any unusual-shaped object.

The pattern is in two halves, which are not identical. You will need to trace the whole of the left-hand side first. Then place the broken line of the right-hand pattern on the broken line of the left-hand pattern and trace the remaining pattern lines on the right-hand side.

Only four basic colours have been used for this design.

Techniques
Basic brush strokes
Dots
Tipping
Double loading
Basic crescent

Brushes
D77 Nos. 3, 6 and 8 (D88 ¼-in (6-mm) can be
  substituted for an 8)
D88 ¼-in (6-mm) and ⅜-in (10-mm)
D99 Nos 1 and 4

Palette
Cadmium Red Deep
Yellow Ochre
Payne's Grey
Titanium White
wine: Cadmium Red Deep + touch Payne's Grey
pink: Titanium White + touch wine
dark brown: wine + touch more Payne's Grey
grey: Titanium White + touch Payne's Grey

Painting instructions

Follow the painting instructions in conjunction with the steps in the colour illustration.

1 For the leaves:
A Load the D88 ⅜-in (10-mm) brush with grey and paint one large 'S' stroke for each 'S' shaped leaf.
B Load the D77 No. 6 brush and paint a comma stroke for each smaller leaf.
C Load the D88 ⅜-in (10-mm) brush and paint one comma stroke and one 'S' stroke for each large leaf.
Load the D99 No. 1 brush with Titanium White, pick up a little grey on the brush and overstroke the leaves in A, B and C.

STEP-BY-STEP GUIDE TO PAINTING BAVARIAN FLOWERS AND BIRD

Open tulip

Carnation

Leaves

Rose

Bud

Yellow flower

Bird

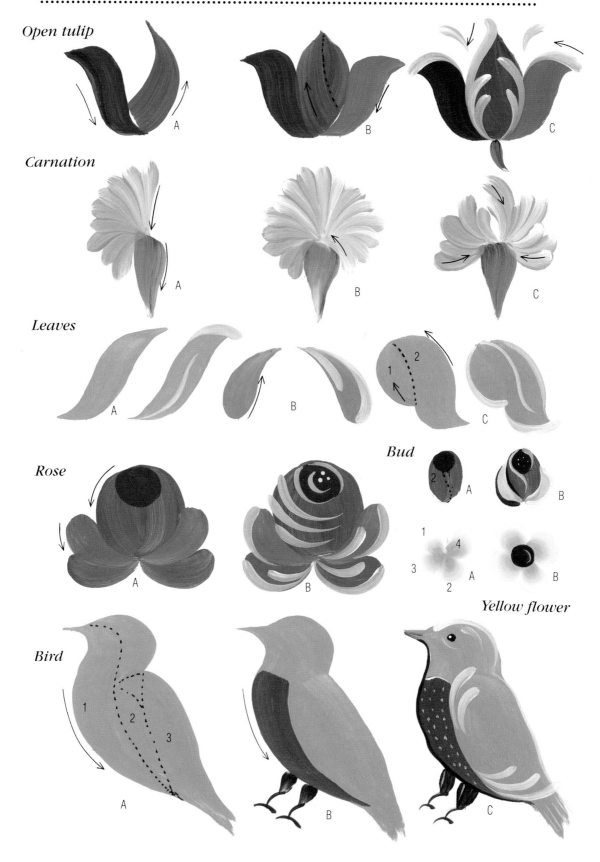

FIG. 69

2 For the calyx and stalk of the carnation, load the D88 ⅜-in (10-mm) brush with grey tipped with Payne's Grey and paint one straight stroke. Use the D77 No. 3 brush for the tulip stalks. For other stalks, use the D99 No. 1 brush loaded with grey.

3 When painting the tulips, do not wash the brush between loading.

A Load the D88 ⅜-in (10-mm) brush with Payne's Grey, dip into a little Cadmium Red Deep and paint an 'S' stroke for the left-hand petal. Turn the design upside down. Add more Cadmium Red Deep to the brush and paint one comma stroke.

B Load the brush with the same colour and paint another comma stroke. Turn the work to its original position and load the brush, picking up a touch more Titanium White, and paint the right-hand petal.

C Load the D99 No. 4 brush with Titanium White which has picked up a little of the petal colour on the brush and paint overstrokes.

4 When painting the carnations, do not wash the brush between loading.

A Load the D77 No. 6 brush with Yellow Ochre and paint a few comma stroke petals on the left-hand side. Paint a few more petals working in a clockwise direction, but each time tip the brush with Titanium White, making a gradual change in colour.

B Paint one straight stroke for the centre petal and continue round clockwise, tipping the brush for each stroke.

C Load as for A, but follow the shape of the flower.

5 When painting the roses, do not wash the brush between loading.

A Load the D88 ⅜-in (10-mm) brush with wine and paint one large circle using 'C' strokes. Load the D77 No. 8 with wine, picking up a little Titanium White to make the paint a fraction lighter in colour, then paint four comma strokes at the base of the rose, starting with the two bottom petals. Load the D88 ¼-in (6-mm) brush

with dark brown and paint a small circle on the large one.

B Load the D99 No. 1 brush with Titanium White, picking up a little pink, and paint overstrokes.

6 For the rose buds:

A Load the D88 ¼-in (6-mm) brush with wine and paint an oval shape by painting two comma strokes. Load the D77 No. 3 brush with dark brown and paint a small circle on the oval.

B Reverse your work and load the D77 No. 3 brush with Titanium White which has picked up a little pink. Paint two comma strokes at the base of the bud. Load the D99 No. 1 brush with Titanium White and paint overstrokes. Load the D99 No. 1 brush with Payne's Grey and paint overstrokes.

7 For the yellow flowers:

A Double load the D88 ⅜-in (10-mm) brush with Yellow Ochre and Titanium White and paint four basic crescent strokes.

B When dry, load the D77 No. 3 brush with Payne's Grey and paint the flower centre. When dry, load the D99 No. 1 brush with Titanium White and paint a tiny 'C' stroke.

8 For the bird:

A Load the D88 ⅜-in (10-mm) brush with grey and paint the bird with three 'S' strokes.

B Load the D88 ⅜-in (10-mm) brush with wine and paint one comma stroke for the breast. Load the D88 ¼-in (6-mm) brush with Payne's Grey and paint two straight strokes for the legs.

C Load the D99 No. 1 brush with Payne's Grey and paint two comma strokes for the base of the legs and the feet. Load the D99 No. 1 brush with Titanium White and paint overstrokes. Load the D99 No. 1 brush with Payne's Grey and outline the breast. Load the D99 No. 1 brush with Yellow Ochre and paint one straight stroke for the beak.

9 Paint all the dots.

PROJECT 12
Hindelooper
········

In this rendition of Hindelooper I have tried to keep things simple. This form of painting is very much for the freehand artist as there is plenty of line work and overstrokes. I know that watercolour artists will enjoy this pattern as they can have fun 'fiddling' with all those overstrokes! Like the Pennsylvania Dutch design in Project 20, this painting can look dull until you reach the final stages when the line work and overstrokes are added.

The clogs were prepared as for bare wood and painted in medium slate blue. As there is only one pattern and two clogs, the pattern has to be reversed for the second clog.

You will notice a touch of Payne's Grey has been added to the majority of colours to tone them down, and the Hindeloopen dots are painted with brush hairs.

Techniques
Basic brush strokes
Basic crescent
Dry brushing

Brushes
D77 Nos 3 and 6
D88 ¼-in (6-mm)
D99 No. 1

Palette
Yellow Ochre
Payne's Grey
red: Cadmium Red Deep + touch Payne's Grey
brown: red + touch more Payne's Grey
blue: Indanthrene Blue + Payne's Grey
cream: Titanium White + Yellow Ochre
green: Yellow Ochre + Indanthrene Blue

Painting instructions

Follow the painting instructions in conjunction with the steps in the colour illustration (page 104).

1 For the tulips:
A Load the D77 No. 6 brush with Yellow Ochre and paint one straight stroke.
B Reload and paint two comma strokes.
C When dry, load the D99 No. 1 brush with brown and paint overstrokes.
D Load the D99 No. 1 brush with cream and paint four comma strokes.

2 For the pods (the colours for the top pair of pods are given in brackets):
A Load the D77 No. 6 brush with Yellow Ochre (red) and paint two comma strokes to form an oval shape.
B Load the D88 ¼-in (6-mm) brush with brown (blue) and paint one wide 'C' stroke.

STEP-BY-STEP GUIDE TO PAINTING HINDELOOPER

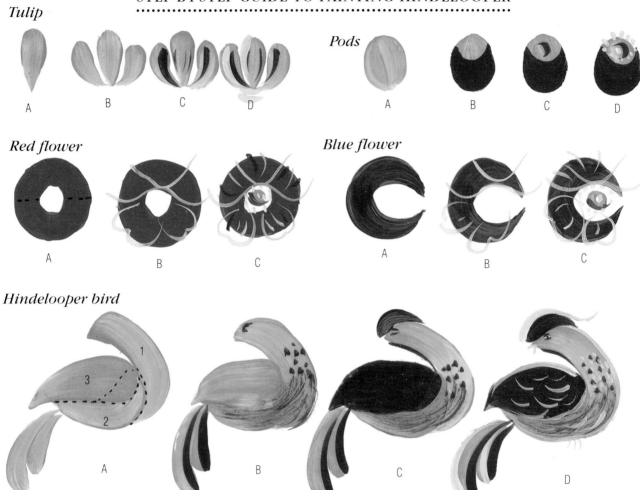

Tulip

Pods

Red flower

Blue flower

Hindelooper bird

C Load the D99 No. 1 brush with brown
(blue) and paint one small 'C' stroke.

D Load the D99 No. 1 brush with cream
(cream) and paint dots.

3 For the red flower (full circle):

A Load the D88 ¼-in (6-mm) brush with red
and paint one crescent brush stroke. Paint
the second crescent directly on top of the
first but facing the opposite direction, thus
forming a circle.

B Load the D99 No. 1 brush with cream and
paint line work.

C Load the D99 No. 1 brush with Yellow
Ochre and paint the flower centre.
Continue painting the centre by loading

the D99 No. 1 brush with brown and
painting tiny comma strokes. Continuing
with the same brush, paint brown overstrokes and cream dots.

4 For the blue flower (half-circle):

A Load the D88 ¼-in (6-mm) brush with blue
and paint one crescent brush stroke.
Continue as for step 3 above, parts B and C.

5 For the Hindelooper bird:

A Load the D88 ¼-in (6-mm) brush with
Yellow Ochre and paint three comma
strokes for the wing and body. Load the
D77 No. 3 brush with Yellow Ochre and
paint two comma strokes for the tail.

FIG. 70

B When dry, load the D77 No. 3 brush with brown and paint two comma strokes for the tail. Then, with the D99 No. 1 brush, paint the eyes and brown marks below the neck. Load a dry brush with brown and dry brush the bird's breast in the direction shown.

C Load the D88 ¼-in (6-mm) brush with blue and paint two comma strokes for the wing feathers. Load the D77 No. 3 brush with blue and paint a comma stroke for the head. Load the D99 No. 1 brush with brown and paint a line stroke under the neck.

D Load the D99 No. 1 brush with cream and paint comma strokes on the tail and over-strokes on the wing, crest and breast and

mark the beak. Paint dots to the breast and a highlight to the eye.

For steps 6, 7 and 8, refer to the photograph on page 103.

6 For the leaves, load the D77 No. 3 brush with green and paint one comma stroke. Load the D99 No. 1 brush with cream and paint overstrokes.

7 Load the D99 No. 1 brush with cream and paint the stalks.

8 Paint the remaining two curving, flowing brush strokes by loading the D99 No. 1 brush with brown. Repeat using cream.

PROJECT 13
Fuchsia
·······

Fuchsias come in many shapes, sizes and colours. I have chosen burgundy and pink for the fuchsias on the chest of drawers. The pattern was designed to fit the small drawer, but as you can see from the colour photograph on page 107 each drawer is a different height, starting with a small drawer at the top and increasing in height towards the bottom. To overcome this problem I added extra leaves to the third drawer and, for the bottom drawer, I painted four 'S' strokes for ribbons to make the pattern wider.

The chest of drawers was prepared as for painted wood and painted in light and dark shades of pine green.

To transfer the whole pattern, trace the lines of the pattern, then fold the pattern in half on the broken line and trace the lines that remain on the other half.

Techniques
Basic brush strokes
Dots
Tipping
Floating colour
Dry brushing
Stippling
Dipped crescent
Ruffled crescent
Pointed crescent
Sponge pollen effect for flower centres

Brushes
D77 Nos 3 and 6
D88 ¼-in (6-mm) and ⅜-in (10-mm)
D99 No. 1
No. 0 liner
Stencil brush for stippling

Palette
Burnt Umber
Titanium White
Gold
burgundy: Permanent Rose + touch Payne's Grey
medium pink: burgundy + touch Titanium White
light pink: medium pink + touch more Titanium White
dark green: Opaque Oxide of Chromium + touch Payne's Grey
light green: dark green + Titanium White
light grey: Titanium White + touch Payne's Grey

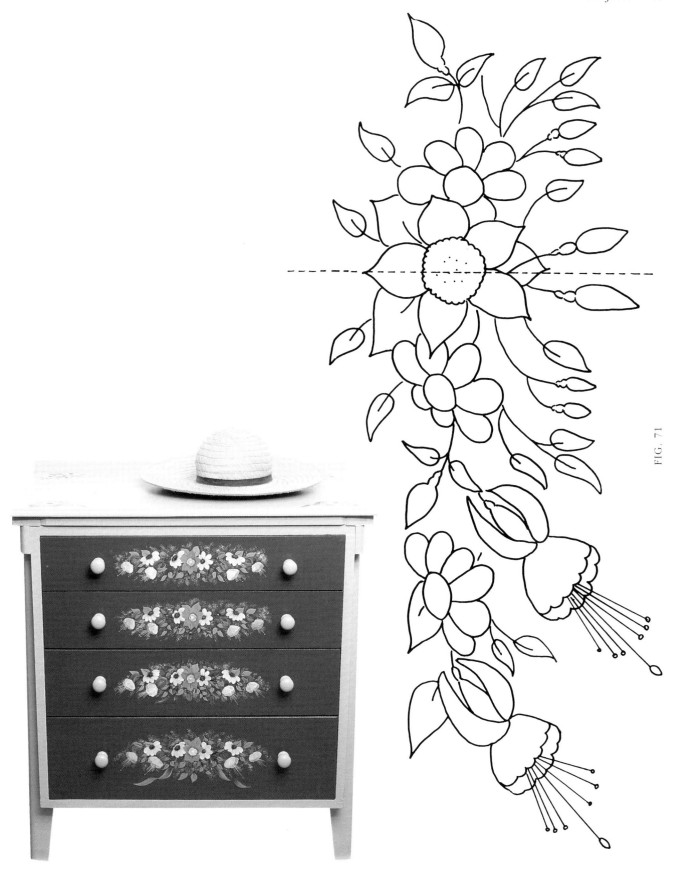

FIG. 71

Painting instructions

Stipple the background in dark green, Titanium White and burgundy around the outside edge of the flowers and leaves.

1 To paint the small leaves, load the D77 No. 6 brush with light green and paint straight and comma strokes.

2 Load the D88 ¼-in (6-mm) brush with light green and paint the remaining leaves using comma and 'S' strokes as in Project 3, step 1A. Avoid painting under the fuchsia petals as the brush strokes will show through the petals.

3 Load the D77 No. 6 brush with medium pink tipped with burgundy and paint one straight stroke for the calyx of the fuchsia starting at the stalk end and finishing at the petals.

4 To paint the fuchsia buds, load the D77 No. 6 brush with medium pink and tip with burgundy for each stroke. Paint all the buds with one straight stroke, varying the pressure.

5 Load the D77 No. 3 brush with light green, tip with burgundy and paint one tiny straight stroke (with pressure) at the base of the calyx and the base of each bud. Start from the flower end and paint towards the stalk.

FIG. 72

6 For the daisy petals, load the D77 No. 6 brush with light grey tipped with Titanium White for each stroke. Paint comma and straight strokes.

7 For the fuchsia petals, load the D88 ⅜-in (10-mm) brush with medium pink and paint one flower at a time. Refer to Fig. 72 and paint one row of three closed dipped crescent strokes for the petals. Before the paint dries, add another row by loading the brush with light pink and painting three slightly shorter, closed dipped crescents on top of the first row.

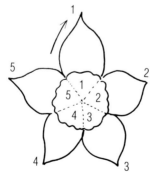

FIG. 73

8 Continuing with the fuchsia, load the D88 ¼-in (6-mm) brush with medium pink, tipped with burgundy, and paint two comma strokes, slightly overlapping the beginning of the petals painted in step 7 above.

9 Load the No. 0 liner brush with dark green and paint all the stalks and veins.

10 For the daisy centres, load the D77 No. 6 brush with Burnt Umber and a touch of retarder and paint as for dry brushing flower centres.

11 When dry, sponge the daisy centres lightly with gold to resemble pollen.

12 Follow Fig. 73 for the central five-petalled flower. Load the D88 ⅜-in (10-mm) brush with medium pink and paint pointed crescent strokes in numerical order, starting at the centre of the flower.

While the paint is still wet, continue painting this flower by loading the D88 ¼-in (6-mm) brush with light pink and painting five closed ruffled crescents.

13 Returning to the fuchsia, for the central pistil load the No. 0 liner brush with Titanium White. Paint one long, fine, straight stroke (paint one stroke first on the palette to remove excess paint), pulling outwards from the centre of the flower. Paint the pistil end Titanium White.

14 Paint the fuchsia stamens in medium pink in the same manner. Paint the anthers (on the end of the stamens) in burgundy.

15 Working on the central flower again, using floating colour, load the D88 ⅜-in (10-mm) brush with burgundy and shade around the central ruffled crescents.

16 Still on the central flower, paint the dots in burgundy and Titanium White.

Note: If you have added a ribbon, load the D88 ⅜-in (10-mm) brush with medium pink and tip with burgundy. Paint four 'S' strokes as in Project 2, step 6.

PROJECT 14
Sweet peas
············

Sweet peas come in many shades of mauve, white, pink and red, so choose colours to suit your background. The sweet peas on the planter have been painted using various pinks and mauves. These shades are obtained by mixing together Permanent Rose and Permanent Violet by loading varying amounts of each colour on one side of the brush, with white paint on the other side. The colours need to be blended well on the palette.

The planter was prepared as for rusty metal and painted in a pastel shade of green. The oval shape only was traced from the pattern on to the painted surface and then painted using a flat synthetic-haired brush loaded with cream. Two coats of paint were necessary. The inside of the oval was then marbled using a wash of Yellow Ochre paint and allowed to dry thoroughly before receiving a coat of varnish and the rest of the pattern.

Techniques
Basic brush strokes
Tipping
Double loading
Floating colour
Tendrils
Stippling
Ruffled crescent

Brushes
D77 No. 3
D88 ¼-in (6-mm) and ⅜-in (10mm)
D99 Nos. 1 and 4
Stencil brush for stippling

Palette
Permanent Violet
Permanent Rose
Titanium White
Yellow Ochre
cream: Titanium White + touch Yellow Ochre
dark green: Hooker's Green + Payne's Grey
medium green: Opaque Oxide of Chromium +
   touch Payne's Grey + touch Titanium White
light green: medium green + Titanium White

FIG. 74

Painting instructions

1 Stipple around the outline of the pattern only in dark green. Stipple again in Yellow Ochre and Titanium White.

2 Depending on the leaf size, load either the D88 ⅜-in (10-mm) brush or ¼-in (6-mm) brush with medium green and paint all the leaves using comma and 'S' strokes, as in Project 3, step 1A. Avoid painting under the sweet pea petals.

3 When dry, repeat step 2 above to produce a denser colour.

4 Load the D99 No. 4 brush with light green and paint curls on the leaves with 'shaky' comma or straight strokes, as shown in the colour illustration.

5 Load the D99 No. 1 brush with light green and paint veins on the leaves. Paint the tendrils.

6 For the sweet peas, use various shades of pink and mauve by mixing together Permanent Violet and Permanent Rose in different quantities.

　Double load the D88 ⅜-in (10-mm) brush with the chosen colour on one side and with Titanium White on the other side. Paint three ruffled crescents for the petals, using pressure to spread the brush well, as in Fig. 75. The leading colour will be the chosen colour.

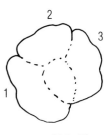

FIG. 75

Reload the D88 ⅜-in (10-mm) brush (or the D88 ¼-in (6-mm) brush for slightly smaller sweet peas) with the same colours as before and paint two more small ruffled crescents in the centre of the flower as shown in Fig. 76.

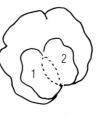

FIG. 76

　Continue to paint all the sweet peas as above, loading the brush with a slightly different shade for each flower.

7 Double load the D88 ⅜-in (10-mm) brush as for the petals and paint three closed ruffled crescent strokes for the buds, as shown in Fig. 77.

8 Load the D77 No. 3 brush with cream, tip with pink/mauve and paint one comma stroke in the centre of the flower.

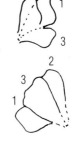

FIG. 77

9 Load the D99 No. 1 brush with light green and paint two comma strokes under the flower bud petals and at the base of all the sweet pea flowers.

10 Load the D88 ⅜-in (10-mm) brush with dark green as for floating colour. Paint shading on the leaves next to the leaf curl and next to the petals as shown in the colour illustration.

PROJECT 15
Poppies and corn
••••••••••••••••

The style of painting and pattern form in this project is reminiscent of folk designs found in farming areas of Germany. The delicate texture of the poppy is achieved by shading and highlighting with floating colour.

The coal hod was prepared as for rusty metal and then painted blue with a rust inhibitor. The edges of the hod were lightly sprayed with gold paint.

The pattern is in two sections. Place the broken lines on the pattern on top of each other to trace the whole pattern.

Techniques
Basic brush strokes
Dots
Tipping
Floating colour
Sponge pollen effect for flower centres

Brushes
D77 Nos. 3 and 6
D88 ¼-in (6-mm) and ⅜-in (10-mm)
D99 Nos. 1 and 4

Palette
Hooker's Green
Cadmium Yellow Deep
Yellow Ochre
Burnt Sienna
Payne's Grey
Cadmium Red Deep
Gold (Yellow Ochre can be substituted)
white: Titanium White + touch Burnt Umber
poppy red: Vermilion (Hue)
light poppy: Vermilion (Hue) + touch Cadmium
   Yellow Deep + touch white
leaf green: Hooker's Green lightly mixed with
   Cadmium Yellow Deep
light green: leaf green + touch white
light grey: Payne's Grey + white
cream: Titanium White + touch Yellow Ochre

Painting instructions

Follow the painting instructions in conjunction with the steps in the colour illustrations (pages 116–17). The letters in brackets in the instructions refer to the letters on the illustrations.

1 Load the D88 ¼-in (6-mm) brush with leaf green and paint all the leaves (F) using 'S' and comma strokes.

2 Load the D99 No. 1 brush with light green and paint all the stalks and veins on the leaves (F).

3 Load the D88 ⅜-in (10-mm) brush with leaf green tipped with Hooker's Green and paint a straight stroke underneath each white daisy for the calyx (K).

4 Load the D77 No. 6 brush with Cadmium Yellow Deep tipped with Burnt Sienna and paint the buttercup petals with two comma strokes and one straight stroke (H and I).

FIG. 78

STEP-BY-STEP GUIDE TO PAINTING POPPIES AND CORN

Poppy 1

A

B

Poppy 2

A

B

Poppy 3

A

B

Corn

E

Leaf

F

Grass

G

Buttercup

H

I

C

D

C

D

C

D

Daisy

J

K

L

M

5 Load the D77 No. 3 brush with leaf green and paint a 'C' stroke underneath the buttercup petals (I).

6 For the white daisy, load the D99 No. 4 brush with light grey and paint one circle of petals for the open flower and a partial circle for the buds, using 'S' and comma strokes: aim to make the petals dishevelled-looking (J and L).

7 Continuing with the daisy, load the D99 No. 4 brush with white and paint another circle of petals in between the petals on the row underneath (K and M). Paint the drooping petals on the buds (K).

8 Load the D88 ¼-in (6-mm) brush with Burnt Umber and paint 'C' strokes for the daisy centres (M).

9 When painting the corn, load the D77 No. 6 brush with Cadmium Yellow Deep and tip into Burnt Umber. Paint straight strokes starting at the tip and working down the stem, making sure that each stroke is overlapped (E).

10 Load the D99 No. 1 brush with cream and paint whiskers on the corn, pulling outwards from the top of each straight stroke (E).

11 For the grass, use a very fine sponge tipped with white and dab lightly in a circular motion to form the tiny flowers (G).

12 For the daisy centres (M), use the sponge pollen effect with Cadmium Yellow Deep and paint dots with a cocktail stick in Cadmium Yellow Deep. Paint white dots on the grass flowers using a cocktail stick (G).

Poppies
All four poppies can be painted at the same time, but remember that there are three different styles involved (numbered 1, 2 and 3 in the colour illustrations on pages 116–17). Looking at the project pattern sheet (Fig. 78) with the four poppies on it, the top poppy is in style number 3, the two middle poppies are in style number 2, and the bottom poppy is in

style number 1. Each style of poppy has four steps (A to D) running across the colour illustrations. Follow these steps as you paint each different style of poppy.

Look at step A for each style. Use the diagrams as a basis for your brush strokes in building up a completely coloured poppy. Follow the arrow guides shown in step A as you paint in the poppy face, filling in any missing areas with straight brush strokes from petal edge to flower centre. Your final result should look like step B before the white tracing lines have been done.

1 Load the D88 ⅜-in (10-mm) brush with poppy red and paint the petals on all four poppies, using comma and straight strokes.

2 The poppy base petals need two coats; so, when dry, repeat step 1.

3 When dry, use the pattern again to trace the inside lines of the poppy petals on to each flower (B). Take care to identify the correct style of poppy.

4 Load the D88 ⅜-in (10-mm) brush with Cadmium Red Deep as for floating colour and shade the poppies (C). The colour side of the brush will be against the white traced line, and you need to check which side of the line by referring to (C) where the colour effects are displayed.

5 Load the D88 ⅜-in (10-mm) brush with light poppy as for floating colour and add highlights to the poppies (D) using the highlighted areas shown as a guide.

6 For poppy style 1, load the D88 ¼-in (6-mm) brush with Payne's Grey and carefully paint the centre using 'C' strokes (D).

For poppies style 2 and 3, load the D77 No. 3 brush with Payne's Grey and fill in the centre carefully (D).

Load the D99 No. 1 brush with Payne's Grey (wiping off excess paint) and add stamens to the poppies (D). Paint from the centre of the flower outwards.

For the pollen, sponge the centre with a touch of Gold or Yellow Ochre (D).

Projects 119

PROJECT 16
Rosemaling
•••••••

This ornamental cheese platter is similar to platters found in Norway. The rosemaling design is my interpretation of Rogaland rosemaling, symmetrical with strong colours, intricate flowers and solid but varied line work.

The paint needs to be of a good flowing consistency to enable you to paint long brush strokes. Flowing medium added to the paint can prove helpful. A smooth and unblemished surface will improve your scroll work.

The wooden platter (page 121) was prepared as for bare wood and painted in a red clay base coat.

The scrolls are painted using three brush strokes. The large main scroll is painted first, followed by the smaller secondary scroll and, finally, a comma stroke is painted at the beginning of the first scroll. The highlights on the inside of the scrolls are painted with floating colour.

Techniques
Basic brush strokes
Dots
Tipping
Double loading
Floating colour
Cross-hatching
Scrolls
Basic crescent

Brushes
D77 No. 6
D88 ¼-in (6-mm) and ⅜-in (10-mm)
No. 0 liner

Palette
Titanium White
Payne's Grey
Yellow Ochre
Burnt Sienna
beige: Titanium White + touch Burnt Sienna
green: light turquoise + Yellow Ochre
light turquoise: Turquoise + Titanium White
medium blue: light turquoise + Payne's Grey
dark blue: Payne's Grey + Turquoise
pink: Permanent Rose + Titanium White

FIG. 79

FIG. 80

FIG. 81

Painting instructions

1 For the scrolls, follow Fig. 80. Load the D88 ⅜-in (10-mm) brush with light turquoise and paint the main scroll (A). Load the D88 ¼-in (6-mm) brush for the secondary scroll (B). Load the D88 ⅜-in (10-mm) brush for the comma stroke (C) at the beginning of the main scroll.

2 For the small crescent flowers, double load the D88 ¼-in (6-mm) brush with medium blue and Titanium White. Paint five closed crescent brush strokes. Paint a Yellow Ochre dot for each centre.

3 For the leaves, load the D77 No. 6 brush with green tipped with Yellow Ochre and paint three comma strokes, working carefully to avoid painting under the large white flower.

4 For the large white flower, load the D88 ⅜-in (10-mm) brush with beige and paint eight closed and elongated crescent brush strokes, starting at the centre of the flower. When dry, load the D88 ¼-in (6-mm) brush with pink and paint five closed crescent brush strokes.
   Load the No. 0 liner brush with Burnt Sienna tipped with pink and paint three straight strokes on each petal.
   Load the No. 0 liner brush with Titanium White and outline the petals. Paint the large central dot in dark blue.

5 Load the D88 ⅜-in (10-mm) brush with Titanium White as for floating colour and highlight the inside edge of all the scrolls.

6 Load the No. 0 liner brush with light turquoise and paint comma strokes on the inside of the scrolls.

7 Load the No. 0 liner brush with dark blue and outline the scrolls, varying the pressure on the brush. Paint one brush stroke starting from the back of the scroll and painting forwards, finishing round the 'knob' end of the

scroll. Rejoining the beginning of this brush stroke, paint the second stroke towards the pattern centre (see Fig. 81). Continuing with dark blue, paint all the remaining brush strokes and cross-hatching.

8 Load the No. 0 liner brush with Titanium White tipped with pink and paint the five remaining straight strokes on the outside of the scrolls.

9 For the border, load the No. 0 liner brush with light turquoise and paint small 'S' strokes. Load the No. 0 liner brush with pink and paint two small comma strokes between each 'S' stroke.

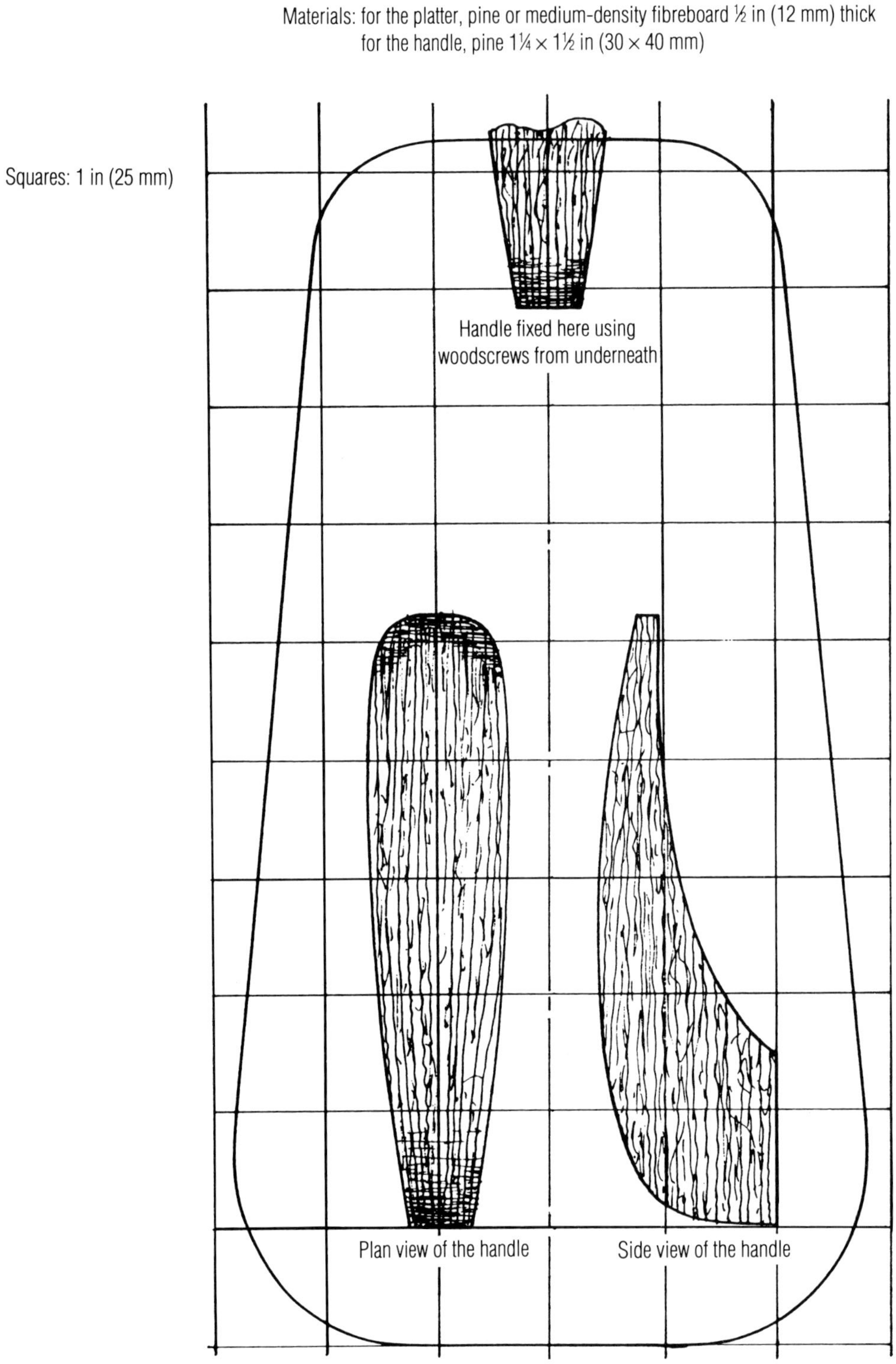

Materials: for the platter, pine or medium-density fibreboard ½ in (12 mm) thick
for the handle, pine 1¼ × 1½ in (30 × 40 mm)

Squares: 1 in (25 mm)

Handle fixed here using
woodscrews from underneath

Plan view of the handle   Side view of the handle

FIG. 82
Woodwork pattern for the cheese platter

PROJECT 17
Clematis
....

The closed elongated pointed crescent brush stroke makes a perfect petal shape for the clematis.

This small table not only required a coat of paint, but also the legs were straight and needed to be turned on a lathe to make them more interesting. The table was prepared as for painted wood in a red clay colour. The background effect was achieved by using the sponging technique: Burnt Umber and Burnt Sienna were used together on a piece of sponge, allowed to dry and then a wash of Payne's Grey was brushed across the surface.

The colour illustration shows a stippled area around the pattern and a gold band has also been added. The stippling has been omitted on the table and white dots added.

To trace the whole design from the book, make sure that the tracing paper is large enough to trace the entire circle. Fold the tracing paper in half and place the fold line of the paper on the broken line on the pattern. Trace one half of the pattern. Remove the tracing paper and turn 180 degrees (do not reverse the pattern), so that the fold line is again on top of the broken line indicated on the pattern, then trace the corresponding pattern.

Techniques
Basic brush strokes
Dots
Double loading
Floating colour
Tendrils and scrolls
Stippling
Basic crescent

Brushes
D88 ¼-in (6-mm) and ⅜-in (10-mm)
D99 No. 3
No. 0 liner
Stencil brush for stippling

Palette
Burnt Sienna
Yellow Ochre
Vermilion (Hue)
Cadmium Yellow
Gold
white: Titanium White + touch Burnt Umber
dark green: Cadmium Yellow Deep + Indanthrene Blue + touch white
medium green: dark green + more white
light green: medium green + more white
blue: white + Indanthrene Blue + touch Burnt Umber
light blue: blue + touch more white
clematis pink: Vermilion (Hue) + Yellow Ochre + white
orange: clematis pink + Burnt Sienna
cream: Yellow Ochre + white

FIG. 83

Enlarge worksheet 109% on a copier before tracing

Painting instructions

Load the stippling brush with white and Yellow Ochre and stipple around the pattern.

1 Load the D88 ¼-in (6-mm) brush with medium green and paint all the small leaves using comma and 'S' strokes.

Load the D88 ⅜-in (10-mm) brush with medium green and paint all the large leaves using comma and 'S' strokes, as in Project 3, step 1A.

2 Load the No. 0 liner brush with light green and paint all the stalks, veins and the leaf turns.

3 For the yellow flowers, double load the D88 ¼-in (6-mm) brush with cream and Cadmium Yellow and paint one closed crescent stroke for each petal with the cream paint leading. Start each petal in the centre of the flower.

Load the D88 ¼-in (6-mm) brush with Yellow Ochre and paint two tiny 'C' strokes (or one dot) for the centre of each flower. Load the No. 0 Liner brush with cream and paint 'C' strokes on the outside edge of all the yellow flower petals. Paint gold dots around the centre of each flower.

4 For the clematis, paint the flowers one at a time, starting with flower A. Paint the petals in numerical order as shown in Fig. 84.

When working on a dark background, it is necessary to undercoat the clematis. This should be done by loading the D88 ⅜-in (10-mm) brush with white. Paint closed elongated pointed crescent brush strokes, starting from the centre of the flower.

When dry, double load the D88 ⅜-in (10-mm) brush with clematis pink and white. With the white paint leading, paint elongated pointed crescent brush strokes, starting from the centre of the flower.

Load the No. 0 liner brush with white and add liner strokes on the outside of all the clematis petals in the same order as the petals were painted.

Load the D88 ¼-in (6-mm) brush with orange and paint 'C' strokes to form the centres of the clematis flowers. Dab each centre with a sponge dipped in cream paint.

Load the No. 0 liner brush with orange and paint very fine, straight strokes for the stamens. Paint dots for the anthers on the end of the stamens with a cocktail stick using Burnt Sienna.

5 For the bluebells, load the D99 No. 3 brush with blue and paint two back-to-back comma strokes.

Load the No. 0 liner brush with light blue and paint an 'S' stroke on one side of each each bluebell.

Paint cream dots under each bluebell using a cocktail stick.

6 For the shading on the leaves, load the D88 ⅜-in (10-mm) brush with dark green as for floating colour.

7 Paint the tendrils in light green.

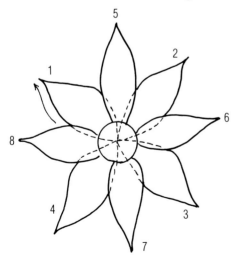

FIG. 84

PROJECT 18
Roses
......

I have painted only three roses and a few buds on this clock as the background has a fake marble appearance. The clock was prepared as for bare wood and painted slate blue and the marbling effect was achieved by washing the surface with white and pink.

The rose flower has been simplified by being broken up into individual petals and you need to practise these before attempting the complete rose. If your first rose looks like a cabbage, don't worry – so did mine! Just keep practising. Once you have learnt the basic techniques for the rose, you can add extra petals, and try different colour variations.

I have used dark green floating colour for shading the leaves and gold for highlighting. The gold gives the leaves an antiqued look.

Here are a few double loading colour suggestions for rose petals – the first of the two colours is the one to use on the outside of the petal (the leading colour on the brush):

Cadmium Yellow and Cadmium Yellow Deep
cream and Cadmium Yellow
Titanium White and very pale green
pink and burgundy
pink and Titanium White
Vermilion (Hue) and Cadmium Yellow

Painting instructions

Use the 'Step-by-step guide to painting rose petals' (pages 128–9) to practise the petal brush strokes first. Then you can experiment with the 'Step-by-step guide to painting roses' to produce a full flower. Finally proceed to the project pattern to paint the full design of roses.

Techniques
Basic brush strokes
Double loading
Floating colour
Rose petal brush strokes (see below)

Brushes
D77 No. 3
Prolene 106 ⅜-in (10-mm)
D88 ¼-in (6-mm) and ⅜ in (10-mm)
No. 0 liner

Palette
Hooker's Green
Permanent Rose
Titanium White
Cadmium Yellow
Gold
dark green: Hooker's Green + Cadmium Yellow
medium green: dark green + touch Titanium White
light green: medium green + more Titanium White
pink: Titanium White + touch Permanent Rose

Step-by-step guide to painting rose petals
Practise numbers 1–8 shown in the guide
opposite in conjunction with the following
instructions.

Use the Prolene 106 ⅜-in (10-mm) brush
and double load with Titanium White and
Permanent Rose.

- **Petal strokes 1 and 7** Paint as for the ruffled
  crescent brush stroke, but remember to
  turn your work for petal 7.
- **Petals 2 and 3** Turn your work sideways
  and paint as you would an 'S' stroke, but
  vary the pressure to form ruffles.
- **Petal 4** Pull the brush towards you on the
  chisel edge with Permanent Rose leading.
  Add pressure while bouncing the brush to
  give a ruffle effect. Gradually release pressure and move the brush away from you
  and on to the chisel edge.
- **Petals 5 and 6** Think of the comma stroke
  when painting these, but instead of adding
  pressure at the beginning of the stroke,
  glide the brush upwards slightly before
  starting the comma. Again vary the pressure to form ruffles.
- **Petal 8** This petal always causes confusion.
  Turn your work so that the right-hand side
  of the rose is nearest to you. Place the
  brush vertically on the chisel edge with the
  second colour leading (Permanent Rose),
  pull the brush towards you, slowly adding
  pressure, then slowly release pressure
  while twisting the brush anti-clockwise,
  finishing on the chisel edge.

FIG. 85

STEP-BY-STEP GUIDE TO PAINTING ROSE PETALS

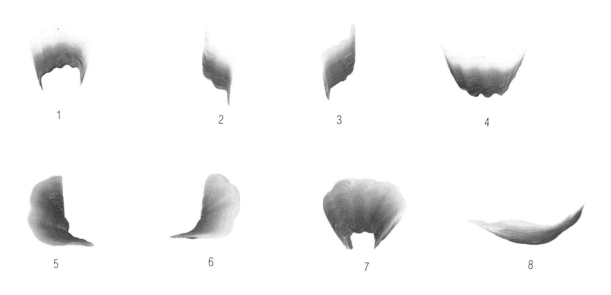

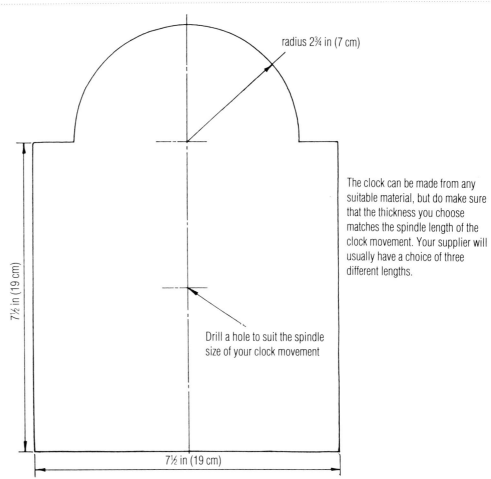

radius 2¾ in (7 cm)

7½ in (19 cm)

7½ in (19 cm)

The clock can be made from any suitable material, but do make sure that the thickness you choose matches the spindle length of the clock movement. Your supplier will usually have a choice of three different lengths.

Drill a hole to suit the spindle size of your clock movement

FIG. 86
Woodwork pattern for the clock

STEP-BY-STEP GUIDE TO PAINTING ROSES

Start at A and work through to L, painting the new brush stroke for each step. Each brush stroke is recognized by a number.

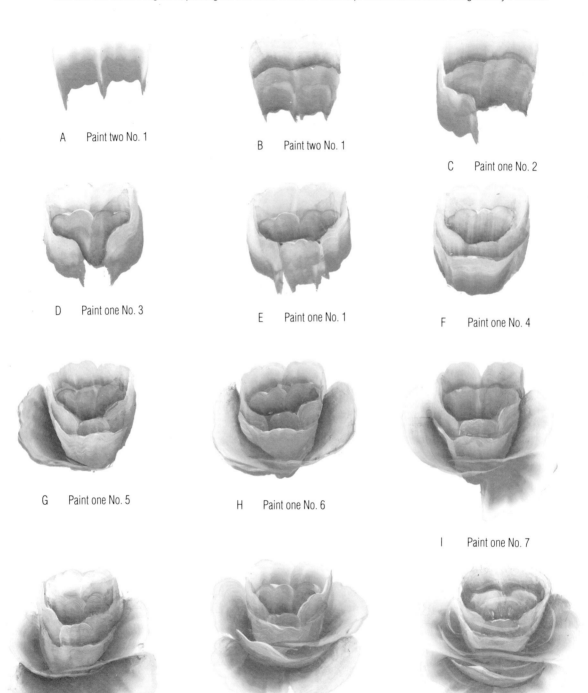

A   Paint two No. 1

B   Paint two No. 1

C   Paint one No. 2

D   Paint one No. 3

E   Paint one No. 1

F   Paint one No. 4

G   Paint one No. 5

H   Paint one No. 6

I   Paint one No. 7

J   Paint one No. 7

K   Paint one No. 8

L   Paint fine lines for petals. Paint stamens

Step-by-step guide to painting roses

When you have mastered the rose petals, you are ready to attempt the whole flower. Each step (A to L) in this guide (page 130) uses a specific stroke from the petal guide above. Refer to the petal guide in each case.

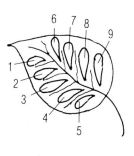

FIG. 87

- To prevent the paint drying while you are painting the rose, smear a thin layer of retarder over the rose shape before beginning.
- Double load the Prolene 106 ⅜-in (10-mm) brush with your chosen colours. Paint the petals in the order indicated in the guide, starting with A and working through to K.
- When painting L, load the No. 0 liner brush with pink for the imaginary petals. Load the No. 0 liner brush with Cadmium Yellow for the stamens.

Painting the project

1 Repeat the techniques from the 'Step-by-step guide to painting roses' to paint the roses in the project pattern.

2 For the rose buds, double load the Prolene 106 ⅜-in (10-mm) brush with Titanium White and Permanent Rose and paint three closed ruffled crescent strokes, painting the two outside petals first.

When dry, paint the sepals. Load the D77 No. 3 brush with dark green and paint two long comma strokes on either side of each bud. Complete by painting one straight stroke in the middle. At the end of these brush strokes allow the brush to shake and wander for effect.

3 For the leaves, load the D88 ¼-in (6-mm) brush with dark green and paint comma and 'S' strokes, as in Project 3, step 1A.

Following Fig. 87, load the D77 No. 3 brush with medium green and paint comma strokes on the leaves. Paint the veins and leaf turns using the No. 0 liner brush and light green paint.

When dry, load the D88 ⅜-in (10-mm) brush with Hooker's Green as for floating colour and paint shading on the leaves around the rose petals. Load the D88 ⅜-in (10-mm) brush with gold as for floating colour and paint highlights on the outside edge of the leaves.

4 For the stalks, use the No. 0 liner brush loaded with light green, adding a touch of pink, and paint stalks. Paint tiny straight strokes for the thorns.

PROJECT 19
Carnation spray
....

Carnations are the perfect choice of flower when painting wedding, anniversary or birthday gifts. Your own personal message can be added to the ribbons.

The box was prepared as for bare wood and painted in a pastel shade of cream to match the pastel shades of these carnations. The reverse stencilling technique was then used: a fern was placed on the lid of the box and sprayed lightly with pastel green so that its (that is, the fern's) edges are scarcely visible. The box was then lined with cream fabric and trimmed with cream lace, though any suitable trimming may be used.

I developed the jagged crescent brush stroke to enable me to paint carnations. The double loading of the brush makes it an ideal stroke for obtaining the coloured edging required for the flowers. I have suggested a few colours for the carnations, but experiment first to find your own preferred colour combination.

The luxurious satin effect on the ribbon is achieved by using floating colour.

Techniques
Basic brush strokes
Dots
Tipping
Double loading
Floating colour
Jagged crescent

Brushes
D77 No. 6
D88 ⅜-in (10-mm)
Prolene 106 ⅜-in (10-mm)
D99 No. 1
No. 0 liner

Palette
Vermilion (Hue)
Cadmium Red Deep
Titanium White
Payne's Grey
Cadmium Yellow
Opaque Oxide of Chromium
light green: Titanium White + touch Opaque Oxide of Chromium + touch Payne's Grey
light pink: Titanium White + touch Cadmium Red Deep
dark pink: light pink + touch Vermilion (Hue)
cream: Titanium White + touch Cadmium Yellow
peach: cream + touch Vermilion (Hue)

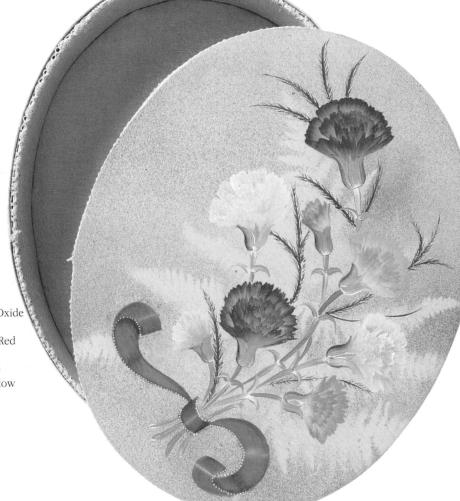

A

B

D

E

B

C

B

D

FIG. 88

Painting instructions

1 For the ferns, load the No. 0 liner brush with Opaque Oxide of Chromium and paint long, flowing strokes for the stalks and tiny strokes for the fronds.

2 Before painting each carnation, wipe the area to be painted with retarder. Paint the carnations using the following colours when
double loading the brush and remember to blend well:
Flower A: Vermilion (Hue) and light pink
Flower B: Titanium White and light green
Flower C: cream and Vermilion (Hue)
Flower D: light pink and Titanium White
Flower E: peach and Titanium White
Load the Prolene 106 ⅜-in (10-mm) brush with the appropriate colour and paint jagged crescent strokes around the top of the flower. Continue painting jagged crescents in the numerical order shown in Fig. 89.

3 For the buds, load the brush as for step 2 above and paint in numerical order as shown in Fig. 90.

4 For the stalks and leaves, load the D99 No. l liner brush with light green and tip with white. Paint comma strokes for the leaves and paint the stalks in sections, reloading the brush for each section. Start at the calyx end of the stalk and work down, as shown in the colour illustration.

5 For the sepals on the calyx, load the D77 No. 6 brush with light green tipped with white and paint comma and straight strokes underneath the carnation petals, as shown in the colour illustration.

6 Now paint the ribbon (See Fig. 91). Load the D88 ⅜-in (10-mm) brush with dark pink and paint the left-hand side of the ribbon with one long comma stroke (A) and one 'C' stroke (B). Paint the right-hand side using two comma strokes (C) and (D).

For the knot, paint one 'C' stroke (E). Load the D88 ⅜-in (10-mm) brush with Vermilion (Hue) as for floating colour and paint shading as indicated by the cross-hatching.

Load the D88 ⅜-in (10-mm) brush with white as for floating colour and paint the highlights 1, 2, 3 and 4. Using the flat side of the brush, paint only back-to-back straight strokes.

Paint white dots on the ribbon edge using a cocktail stick.

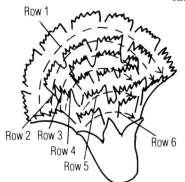

FIG. 89

FIG. 90

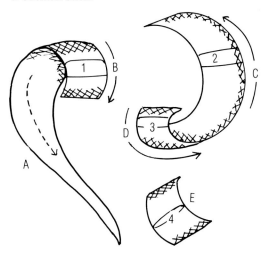

FIG. 91

PROJECT 20
Pennsylvania Dutch
••••••••••••••••••••

T he oval shape of this old fish pan is a pleasing one from a decorative artist's point of view. The pan itself needed much preparation to remove grease and rust. It was prepared for painting as for rusty metals and painted with a black rust inhibitor.

Don't be surprised, when you first start painting this design, if it looks a little drab. Just wait and see the difference when the line work is added. Remember to vary the pressure on the line work to make it more interesting.

Note: When working on black, it is necessary to trace only the outline of the woman as other lines can be traced after undercoating. The man is undercoated only in areas which are not to be painted Payne's Grey.

Techniques
Basic brush strokes
Dots
Cross-hatching
Tendrils and scrolls

Brushes
D77 Nos. 3 and 6
D88 ¼-in (6-mm) and ⅜-in (10-mm)
No. 0 liner

Palette
Payne's Grey
Titanium White
Yellow Ochre
Burnt Umber
pale grey: Titanium White + touch Payne's Grey
cream: Titanium White + touch Yellow Ochre
amber: Yellow Ochre + touch Cadmium Red Deep
light amber: Amber + touch more Titanium White
pink: Titanium White + touch Cadmium Red Deep
country green: Hooker's Green + Yellow Ochre

FIG. 92

Painting instructions

When painting the man and woman, use flat brush strokes to fill in the specific coloured area, keeping the surface as smooth as possible. I have, therefore, given instructions only as to which brush to use and no information on brush strokes.

FIG. 93

1 When undercoating the figures, refer to Fig. 93. Load the D88 ¼-in (6-mm) brush with Titanium White and undercoat the woman, excluding all areas which are to be Payne's Grey. Keep the brush strokes in the direction of the arrows. Undercoat the man in the same manner, again excluding areas to be painted Payne's Grey.

2 When dry, place tracing paper over the couple again and hold in position with masking tape. Push transfer paper gently underneath and trace all the lines which were omitted so that you have guidelines for painting.

3 For the woman, load the D88 ¼-in (6-mm) brush with pink and paint the whole of the head showing below the hat.

Load the D88 ¼-in (6-mm) brush with amber and paint the dress. Repeat this when dry to produce a denser colour.

Load the D88 ¼-in (6-mm) brush with Titanium White and paint the bow in the hair, apron, apron bow, cuff, socks and collar.

Load the D77 No. 3 brush with Payne's Grey and paint the shoes.

Load the D88 ¼-in (6-mm) brush with Payne's Grey and paint the hat.

Load the D77 No. 3 brush with cream and paint the hair.

Load the D77 No. 3 brush with pink and paint the hand.

Load the No. 0 liner brush with pale grey and outline the hat and shoes.

Load the No. 0 liner brush with Burnt Umber and paint the facial features and outline the woman, as shown in the colour illustration.

4 For the man, load the D88 ¼-in (6-mm) brush with pink and paint the face and hands.

Load the D88 ¼-in (6-mm) brush with amber and paint the stockings.

Load the D88 ¼-in (6-mm) brush with Titanium White and paint the cuffs and shirt front.

Load the D88 ¼-in (6-mm) brush with country green and paint the trousers. Repeat this when dry to produce a denser colour.

Load the D88 ¼-in (6-mm) brush with Payne's Grey and paint the jacket, hat and the small area of the belt at the waist.

Load the D77 No. 3 brush with Payne's Grey and paint the shoes.

Load the D77 No. 3 brush with amber and paint the hair.

Load the D77 No. 3 brush with country green and paint the hair bow and cravat.

Paint dots for the buttons using a cocktail stick.

Load the No. 0 liner brush with pale grey and outline the jacket, hat and shoes. Paint the remaining outline and facial features in Burnt Umber as shown in the colour illustration.

Borders

Load the D88 ⅜-in (10-mm) brush with Titanium White and paint the dove. When the

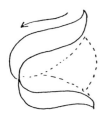

FIG. 94

first coat is dry, repeat in order to produce a denser colour.

Load the D88 ⅜-in (10-mm) brush with Titanium White and undercoat the two tulips by painting two 'S' strokes, as shown in Fig. 94. When the undercoat is dry, repeat this in amber.

Load the No. 0 liner brush with country green and paint all the stalks.

Load the D77 No. 6 brush with country green and paint all the large comma-stroke leaves; use the D77 No. 3 brush for the smaller leaves. Paint the largest leaves with one comma and one 'S' stroke, as in Project 3, step 1A.

FIG. 95

For the two outside flowers, load the D77 No. 6 brush with cream and paint comma strokes for the petals, in numerical order, as shown in Fig. 95. Without washing the brush, load with light amber and paint four more petals on the two inside flowers.

Returning to the tulip, load the D77 No. 6 brush with cream and paint two comma strokes on the inside of the petals, as shown in Fig. 96.

Working on the two bottom groups of leaves, load the D77 No. 6 brush with cream and paint the background for cross-hatching, using straight and comma strokes in numerical order, as shown in Fig. 97.

When dry, load the No. 0 liner brush with country green and cross-hatch and outline the leaves. Paint the comma overstrokes.

Load the No. 0 liner brush with light amber and cross-hatch and outline all the flower centres, as shown in the colour illustration.

Load the D77 No. 3 brush with cream and paint comma strokes above the tulips.

Load the No. 0 liner brush with amber and paint four comma strokes on the two outside flowers.

Load the No. 0 liner brush with cream and paint all the remaining comma strokes on the leaves and flowers. Outline the tulips and paint the scrolls.

Load the No. 0 liner brush with country green and paint six comma strokes for the grass.

Load the No. 0 liner brush with pale grey and paint the line work on the dove.

Paint a large cream dot at the base of the cross-hatched leaves in cream. Paint all the remaining dots in Titanium White using a cocktail stick.

FIG. 96

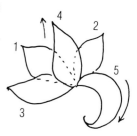

FIG. 97

Daler-Rowney tint chart

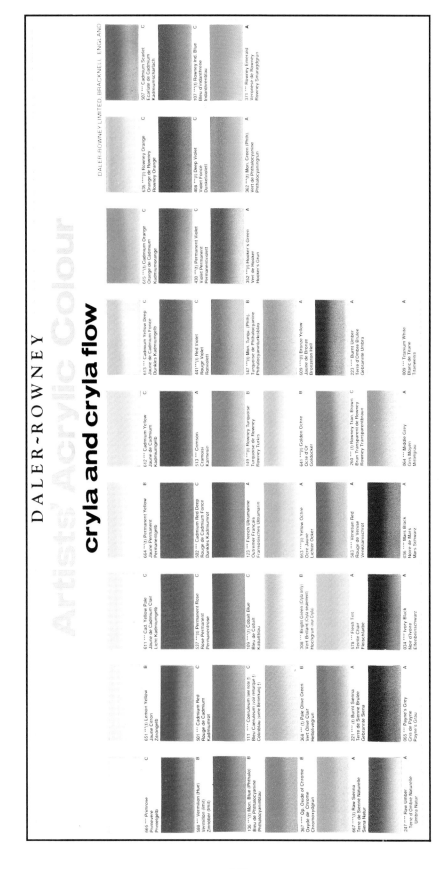

DALER~ROWNEY

Artists' Acrylic Colour

cryla and cryla flow

DALER-ROWNEY LIMITED BRACKNELL ENGLAND

666 *** Primrose
Primevère
Primelgelb · C

655 ***(t) Lemon Yellow
Jaune Citron
Zitronengelb · B

611 *** Cad. Yellow Pale
Jaune de Cadmium Clair
Licht Kadmiumgelb · C

664 ***(t) Permanent Yellow
Jaune Permanent
Permanentgelb · B

612 ***(t) Cadmium Yellow
Jaune de Cadmium
Kadmiumgelb · C

613 ***(t) Cadmium Yellow Deep
Jaune de Cadmium Foncé
Dunkles Kadmiumgelb · C

615 ***(t) Cadmium Orange
Orange de Cadmium
Kadmiumorange · C

636 ***(t) Rowney Orange
Orange de Rowney
Rowney Orange · C

507 *** Cadmium Scarlet
Écarlate de Cadmium
Kadmiumscharlach · C

588 *** Vermilion (Hue)
Vermillon (Imit)
Zinnober (Imit) · B

591 *** Cadmium Red
Rouge de Cadmium
Kadmiumrot · C

537 ***(t) Permanent Rose
Rose Permanent
Permanentrose · C

502 *** Cadmium Red Deep
Rouge de Cadmium Foncé
Dunkles Kadmiumrot · C

513 *** Crimson
Cramoisi
Karmesin · A

441 ***(t) Red Violet
Rouge Violet
Rotviolett · C

430 ***(t) Permanent Violet
Violet Permanent
Permanentviolett · C

408 ***(t) Deep Violet
Violet Foncé
Dunkelviolett · C

107 ***(t) Rowney Ind. Blue
Bleu d'indanthrène
Indanthrenblau · C

136 ***(t) Mon. Blue (Phthalo)
Bleu de Phthalocyanine
Phthalocyaninblau · B

111 *** Cœruleum (see note t)
Bleu Cœruleum (voir remarque t)
Coelinblau (siehe Bemerkung t) · C

109 ***(t) Cobalt Blue
Bleu de Cobalt
Kobaltblau · C

123 *** French Ultramarine
Outremer Français
Französisches Ultramarin · A

147 ***(t) Mon. Turqu. (Phth).
Turquoise de Phthalocyanine
Phthalocyaninturkisblau · B

149 ***(t) Rowney Turquoise
Turquoise de Rowney
Rowney Turkis · B

362 ***(t) Mon. Green (Phth).
Vert de Phthalocyanine
Phthalocyaningrun · A

371 *** Rowney Emerald
Veronèse de Rowney
Rowney Smaragdgrun · A

367 *** Op. Oxide of Chrome
Oxyde de Chrome
Chromoxydgrun · B

368 ***(t) Pale Olive Green
Vert Olive Clair
Hellolivegrun · B

308 *** Bright Green (Cryla only)
Vert Brillant (Cryla seulement)
Hochgrun (nur Cryla) · B

663 ***(t) Yellow Ochre
Ocre Jaune
Lichter Ocker · A

641 ***(t) Golden Ochre
Ocre d'Or
Goldocker · A

352 ***(t) Hooker's Green
Vert de Hooker
Hooker's Grun · A

609 ***(t) Bronze Yellow
Jaune de Bronze
Bronzeton Hell · A

667 *** Raw Sienna
Terre de Sienne Naturelle
Sienna Natur · A

221 *** (t) Burnt Sienna
Terre de Sienne Brûlée
Gebrannte Sienna · A

578 *** Flesh Tint
Teinte Chair
Fleischfarbe · A

583 ***(t) Venetian Red
Rouge de Venise
Venezianischrot · A

260 ***(t) Rowney Tran. Brown
Brun Transparent de Rowney
Rowney Transparentbraun · C

223 *** Burnt Umber
Terre d'Ombre Brûlée
Gebrannte Umbra · A

247 *** Raw Umber
Terre d'Ombre Naturelle
Umbra Natur · A

065 *** Payne's Grey
Gris de Payne
Payne's Grau · A

034 **** Ivory Black
Noir d'Ivoire
Elfenbeinschwarz · A

036 **** Mars Black
Noire de Mars
Mars Schwarz · A

064 *** Middle Grey
Gris Moyen
Mittelgrau · A

009 *** Titanium White
Blanc de Titane
Titanweiss · A

Bibliography

Albrecht, Gary
Rosemaling – Reflections on the Art
(Albrecht, 1985)

Blanchard, Roberta
Traditional Tole Painting
(Dover, 1977)

Foster, Scottie
Scottie's Guide to Bauernmalerei
(Foster, 1991)

Kauffman, Henry
Pennsylvania Dutch American Folk Art
(Olde Springfield Shoppe, 1993)

Lewery, A.J.
Narrow Boat Painting
(David and Charles,1974)

Lichten, Frances
Authentic Pennsylvania Dutch Designs
(Dover, 1976)

Netherlands Country Women's Association
Hinderlooper Schilderkunst Voor Amateurs
(Tineke Wieringa, 1980)

Schatz, Claudine
Hallingdal Rosemaling
(Claudine's House, 1978)

Thode, Vi
Rosemaling – Intermediate Rogaland Style Rosemaling
(Zims, 1979)

Index

....